Never Say Die

ADVANCE PRAISE FOR THE BOOK

'Shripal always dreams big and backs it with passion. A man who has played with money all his life took to playing with storytelling, as he ventured into Smaaash, a sports experiential centre. It was great to partner with him at Star, to see this become real with the power of technology. The "never-say-die" attitude shines on'—**Sanjay Gupta, president, Google Asia–Pacific**

'There are visionaries—and then there is Shripal bhai—a man who turns impossibilities into blueprints. I had the privilege of working with Shripal bhai in the early years of his journey, and those experiences left an enduring mark on me. His clarity of thought, fearlessness in execution and relentless pursuit of excellence have taught me lessons that continue to guide me today. Shripal bhai has never walked the beaten path—he creates his own. Whether in finance, film or gaming, he has consistently dared to do what others only dream of. His ability to see possibilities long before the world does is what truly sets him apart. To me, he has been a true source of inspiration and courage. He saw potential in me before I could see it myself and showed me that growth begins the moment you step beyond comfort. For his belief, guidance and the opportunity to learn from him—I remain deeply grateful'—**Madhusudan Kela, founder, MK Ventures**

Never Say Die

My Life in Business and Entrepreneurship

Shripal Morakhia

Founder of SSKI, Sharekhan and Smaaash

PENGUIN

VIKING

An imprint of Penguin Random House

PENGUIN VIKING

Penguin Viking is an imprint of the Penguin Random House group of companies
whose addresses can be found at global.penguinrandomhouse.com

Published by Penguin Random House India Pvt. Ltd
4th Floor, Capital Tower 1, MG Road,
Gurugram 122 002, Haryana, India

Penguin
Random House
India

First published in Penguin Viking by Penguin Random House India 2025

10 9 8 7 6 5 4 3 2 1

This is a non-fiction book. The events and experiences described in this autobiography
are based on the author's personal recollections and the best understanding of his life.
While every effort has been made to present the truth as accurately as possible, certain
names, locations and identifying details may have been changed to protect the privacy
of individuals. The views and opinions expressed are solely those of the author and do
not necessarily reflect those of any organizations or individuals mentioned. The objective
of this book is not to hurt any sentiments or be biased in favour of or against any
particular person, political party, region, caste, society, gender, creed, nation or religion.
The publisher assumes no responsibility for errors, inaccuracies, omissions or any other
inconsistencies herein and is in no way liable for the same.

Please note that no part of this book may be used or reproduced in any manner
for the purpose of training artificial intelligence technologies or systems.

ISBN 9780143470991

Typeset in Adobe Caslon Pro by Manipal Technologies Limited, Manipal
Printed at Thomson Press India Ltd, New Delhi

www.penguin.co.in

Contents

This book contains discussions of sensitive topics, including mental health struggles and suicide. Reader discretion is advised.

Note to the Reader

I penned the book when it was all darkness. I was at the ebb of my life having lost all. I started working when I was eighteen, and at sixty-four, I lost it all—every penny that I made. My house, my shelter, was also snatched away from me. It was especially painful because I had revived the company I founded, taken it to a new high, and at that time, a few officials intoxicated with power and vengeance decided to have the last laugh.

Little did they realize that in the darkness the illusion vanished and I saw the real me, and thus began my journey of being the person I should have been.

It's never too late.

Physically and financially, I may be down, but emotionally, mentally and spiritually, I am strengthened and I know for a fact that my best is yet to come.

Prologue

I was not dead.

The persistent beeps of the machines in the ICU were a sign. I was being pushed to live.

That annoyed me, even in my sedated state. I didn't want to live. Why else would I have swallowed so many sleeping tablets and washed it down with Lizol?

Why was I alive? What was I made of that even a bottle of disinfectant had not killed me?

Maybe it was the prayers of my wife, my daughter and my mother that had saved me.

Maybe—*maybe*—it was just me.

My brain began to work furiously. My nerves were frayed. I wanted to yank out the tubes that kept me hooked to the life support machines around me. I wanted to run back to office to salvage my wrecked business.

I wanted to scream and shout.

How had it come to this?

I had spent most of my life creating one business after another. In that process, I had enjoyed skyrocketing success and taken crashing failures in my stride. I knew the rules of the game. And yet, here I was, in the sunset years of my life—

overwhelmed by trials and tribulations, false accusations and fake claims. In despair, I had tried to take my own life.

As I listened to the harsh beeps of the machines in the ICU, my mind circled around the same question: *How had it come to this?*

I suppose, as we all must, I have to start at the beginning.

1

An Illustrious Family

If the house of the world is dark
Love will find a way to make windows

—Rumi

8 July 1959–1 December 1974

Six weeks before I was supposed to be born, my father was behind the wheel of our family car in Pune. Sitting with him were my then four-year-old sister, and my mother heavily pregnant with me. Out of the blue, the car fishtailed. My father lost control of the steering, and within seconds, the car was brought to a smashing halt by crashing into a banyan tree. My parents and sister were miraculously unscathed, but my mother's condition worried them enough to rush her to hospital.

I was born that night, at fifteen minutes past midnight. It was 8 July 1959, and I was immediately named Shripal after a legendary king of Jain tradition.

My mother suffered none of the agonies of birth. My arrival was smooth, almost swift, in contrast to the rollercoaster earlier.

Looking back, I think the circumstances of my birth are an excellent metaphor for how my life turned out. It would also be a rollercoaster, with jagged ups and downs.

Four years later, my mother was blessed with twins: Shreyas and Shreyans. Unfortunately, Shreyans passed away in a few days. At four-years-old, I don't remember much about that time in my mother's life, and while she grieved his loss, I remained happily oblivious. It was always, as far as I remember, the five of us: my parents, my siblings and me. We were part of a larger joint family that lived together in an old Victorian-style bungalow in Walkeshwar, South Bombay. I was cocooned by the warmth of grandparents, uncles, aunts, cousins and siblings and many of them had a strong influence on my life.

My grandfather, Kantilal Ishwarlal Morakhia Jain, came to Bombay in 1916. He was a simple man from Radhanpur, a tiny village in what is now Gujarat. Back then, most men who migrated from Radhanpur to Bombay became stockbrokers. That sounds odd, but in those days, Radhanpur was starved of adequate formal education. Thus, many men worked in the stock market as one did not need a formal education to have a lucrative career in that field.

My grandfather had had no other option but to migrate to Bombay as his parents had died early. He stayed with a distant relative in the city, and completed his high school education, studying under the glimmer of streetlamps. He was all of eighteen when he married my grandmother. At the wedding, he gave her a set of two gold bangles. The couple started their conjugal life in a one-room *chawl* in Bhuleshwar. The year was 1918. India was pulsating with a new nationalist fervour, led and fanned by the new, rising political star: Mohandas Karamchand Gandhi. The Champaran satyagraha—with indigo cultivators in Bihar pushing back against their iron-fisted bosses—had taken the nation's imagination by storm. As the country moved towards a more vocal national movement, Gandhi began donation drives from the people. During one such drive, my grandfather asked my grandmother to donate her bangles to the cause. She did so without a fuss—such was Gandhi's power and the nobility of Kantilal Ishwarlal.

My grandfather worked hard and soon established himself in the stock market. He then encouraged other men from Radhanpur to migrate to Bombay and join the stock market. In the late 1940s and early fifties, real estate prices in Bombay were not as steep as today. Our Victorian-style bungalow in Walkeshwar was bought for Rs 2 lakh in 1950. The income came from jobbing (buying and selling shares on the same day to make a profit). My grandfather was a successful jobber of the Bombay Stock Exchange through the 1930s and 1940s. He had a golden run for over two decades, working as a market maker on the stock exchange and dealing only with brokers. I remember that he always wore a dhoti and a short-sleeved kurta over which he would wear a long-sleeved kurta and a coat. Near the Old Stock Exchange Building, he would remove his coat and long-sleeved kurta in his office at 100, Apollo Street, before making his way to the ring of the Exchange. Here, he would always stand on the platform, holding a belt at the Century Mills counter. Many brokers in those days would chew paan and tobacco and his kurta was therefore speckled with red stains. After 2 p.m., he faithfully wore the long-sleeved kurta over the short one.

Jobbers were market makers and risk-takers who bought and sold on their accounts, when the stock exchange was still a physical venue. He would sometimes hold a position overnight as a big market maker in IISCO stocks—the Indian Iron and Steel Company, owned by the Goenka Group which also owned the newspaper, the *Indian Express*. The IISCO was later nationalized by the Government of India. However, by the time I was born, this period was way behind him.

Kantilal Ishwarlal was 6 feet 2 inches tall and had a pious aura around him. When he entered the ring, men would stop to stare and hear him out. Luck was on his side as well because if he was buying a stock of a company, it meant that the stock price would increase. Subsequently, if he was selling stock, it would mean that the price would decrease. My grandfather did not know how to analyse the balance sheet of a company, but he was extremely astute when it came to share price movements. Where people draw extensive charts to determine stock movement, he was gifted with a powerful intuition. From the 1930s to the 1950s, the Bombay Stock Exchange had few listed companies and fewer investors. It was known as an *akhada* (literally, wrestling ring) of speculators. Very few regarded shares as a medium of investment. Land, buildings, diamonds and gold were the favourite portfolios of those who were serious about building wealth.

My grandfather did a business of 11,000 to 12,000 shares daily. In the ring, he did not take notes of what was purchased and sold. It was imprinted on his mind. He would come back to his office and note the trades that he had done, whom he had done them with, and at what prices. I think he was blessed by the divine because he lived a pious life.

On the flip side, my grandfather was always bothered by the fact that he was not formally educated. He knew the pitfalls of illiteracy. To make up for it, he built a boarding school in our hometown of Radhanpur. He also donated handsomely to a girls' school in Bombay which exists to date. Named after my grandmother Shakuntala Kantilal Ishwarlal, Jain Girl's High School on Queen's Road was built in 1936. This great man's philanthropy would always be focused on education and he regarded religion as a basis for education. He also lived life king-size and built a palatial home on the beautiful Queen's Necklace that runs along Marine Drive in Bombay, and overlooks the Arabian Sea. It was called Ishwar Niwas and he lived there with his extended family. The home was open to all, especially sadhus and *sadhvis*.

I was not born there. But I was told by my parents that Ishwar Niwas was nothing short of a palace. Our kitchen was open 24 hours a day. Every day, political figures, freedom fighters, and their troops would arrive for lunch or dinner. No Jain sadhu or sadhvi would leave the place till they were served food cooked by my mother and her sisters-in-law. The entire family took great joy in feeding others.

My grandfather's faith in Jainism led him to build a temple inside Ishwar Nivas where outsiders could come and pay their respects. This was according to the Jain concept of *ghar derasar*, a temple situated in the house. The temple was aesthetically built and many would come to pay respect to the Jain *tirthankaras* and *munis*.

Luck ran its princely course through my grandfather's life for two decades. By 1957, the Bombay Stock Exchange had become so lucrative that the Government of India recognized it as India's first stock exchange and gave it official trading rights. On the one hand, this legitimacy attracted investors and traders, but on the other hand, it attracted government intervention and scrutiny. Now, the government tightened its noose around income tax. My grandfather came under the scanner, since he had resorted to the kind of planning and saving methods that were challenged by the income tax department

A case was registered against my grandfather and his relatives. Nani Palkhiwala—the legendary lawyer, known for his expertise in income tax law, who was a novice then—was hired by the family. He was young, just kicking off his career as the in-house lawyer for the Tata Group. My father approached him first, to defend my grandfather. Palkhiwala took on the case and won it—a huge victory, because if we had lost, my grandfather would have had to pay a few crores of rupees back to the government. This sounds mundane today, but I write of the 1950s, when a few crores was an unthinkable amount of money.

The family was thrilled beyond words at this victory. It was no small feat to have won against the income tax department of the Government of India. But strangely, it had the opposite effect on my grandfather who spiralled instead into deep introspection.

Hours later, after we had got the news, my grandfather called for my father and said, 'get me my *dagla topi* (coat and cap). I want to go out. You come with me. Only you will understand me.'

Father and son got into the family's black Buick. As the car pulled out of the driveway and turned into the busy Bombay streets, my grandfather turned to look at my father. His eyes had a crystal-clear gleam. 'Truth,' he said, 'is the basis of my religion. I have built a Jain temple, a boarding school and a girls' school. What is the single most important teaching imparted in these institutions? *TRUTH*. That is the basis of Jainism. Now, should I sacrifice truth for a few crores?'

My father understood.

Kantilal Ishwarlal, a staunch Jain, was going to return the money he owed to the Government of India.

When he was finally sitting in front of the income tax commissioner, my grandfather spoke with a rare combination of humility and confidence. 'I have won the case. But I have lost in my eyes and therefore, in the eyes of god. I do not want this on my conscience. I hereby accept my liability with penalty.'

The cost of this admission was heavy. To pay back the income tax owed and the subsequent penalties levied meant that it was necessary to sell Ishwar Niwas. Surprisingly, a buyer appeared almost overnight—none other than the Sheikh of Kuwait, who flew down personally to sign the deal. From what my parents have told me, the sheikh was mesmerized by the bungalow's architectural splendour. I wasn't surprised. The temple itself was built to resemble the legendary Dev Lok, the heaven in Jain tradition. Sadly, though, Ishwar Niwas was later rechristened to Al Sabbah Court, but it still stands today, overlooking the Arabian Sea as proudly as it always did.

As I write of this incident, I am conflicted. Had this been an overly impulsive decision on my grandfather's part? Who gives away a prime property like Ishwar Niwas? After all, he had won the case against the government!

But on the other hand, one needs to understand that he came from a generation moulded by the freedom struggle. This government of Independent India was an ideal he had not only aspired to, but actually fought for. For him, Gandhiji and Narsi Mehta's lyrics '*Vaishnav Jann toh tene kahiye*', (only he is a man of God who does good to others), the Navkaar mantra of Jainism (a very important chant in Jainism recited while meditating), and the trials and tribulations of the twenty-four Tirthankaras, especially Bhagwan Mahavir, were his biggest influences.

In newly Independent India, my grandfather treated the government as an extended part of the family. Any loss to the government was a loss to him. That is what he thought.

Now, the news had to be broken to the family. My grandfather and father first confided in my mother. She insisted that the head of the family must break the news to everyone else.

Those were the days when the word of elders was respected. Everyone accepted my grandfather's decision without a murmur of protest. Nor was there a word spoken when he said that in addition to the sale of Ishwar Niwas, much of the jewellery had to be sold. Surprisingly, everything was smoothly accomplished in a matter of seven days.

For the next two years, the entire family moved to Colaba and lived on rent. Back then, Colaba was a downtrodden area and the smell of dried fish clogged the salty air. For a Jain family, that didn't even eat onion or garlic, this was sheer torture. Months later, when we could, the family moved to a smaller bungalow—10, Manav Mandir Road in Walkeshwar—built by the legendary Mulji Jetha. My grandfather called it Shakuntal after his wife whom he loved dearly.

I was born in Shakuntal. As a child, I was in awe of my grandfather. Today I realize the value of his integrity and piety in the principles he not only preached, but also practiced. He believed, for instance, in the concept of karma. As you sow, so shall you reap. Through everything, he never forgot his religion. In bad times, we forget our religion and its ethos. He had unwavering faith in Jainism, ahimsa, and karma. Wealth and material things were transient in his eyes. When his second daughter married into a family that wasn't well off, my grandfather allowed it—simply because of their values and their own unquestioned faith in Jainism. He would tell me the same when I was a boy—'wealth comes and goes. I came to Bombay with nothing, yet your grandmother married me. I made wealth, lost it . . . wealth flows, comes, and goes . . . what matters most are values and principles.' He drummed these principles into his grandchildren and we would listen to him with our mouths agape, not understanding a word of what he said.

His wealth diminished over the years, but his generosity never ebbed. My grandfather loved to feed people and our kitchen continued to be open for sadhus, sadhvis and the poor. My grandfather would put food on their plate with a smile and he encouraged his grandchildren to do the same.

As a child, I did not understand, but now as a sixty-five-year-old, I hold deep regard for his profound wisdom. He would always encourage us to feed as many sadhus and sadhvis because there was nothing greater than *anna daan* (donation of food). He believed that one's house should be located such that sadhus and sadhvis could come for *bhiksha* (charity). He welcomed them and ensured their stay was a comfortable one. Notwithstanding his position in life, he never ceased to be a giver.

Because what truly mattered to him was *dharmalaabh*— what are you willing to do for your *dharma*? Practising the values of Jainism was his soul's purpose. And that is what explained his mesmerizing aura. Back then he was the only man I feared out of sheer respect. Sure, I feared my parents and teachers—but that was because they would never spare the rod.

As I reminisce about the times spent with my grandfather, I understand his greatness. I believe this was his last human life and he was unwinding from the *chakravyuh* of life and death.

My grandfather died in 1971. He was seventy-one and I was twelve.

A respected trailblazer, entrepreneur and philanthropist, my grandfather, Kantilal Ishwarlal, at heart was a family man. The day he passed away, the vast network of his Jain joint family was present in full force at Shakuntal, as if everyone, spiritually connected, had flocked to pay final homage to the revered patriarch.

* * *

If my grandfather was Raja Harishchandra, my father was Shri Ram, in my eyes. For him, every wish of his parents was a command to be carried out at all costs. He was so devoted to serving his parents that it resulted in arguments between him and my mother. She was right in the sense that my father was not focused on the business, despite being a genius in his own right. He could have made it bigger than my grandfather if he had wanted to!

Unlike my grandfather his knowledge of the balance sheets of every company was thorough. In fact, when I was fourteen years old, I remember that he predicted a multi-generation bull run on the stock markets! His method of working was different to my grandfather's—he would buy a few shares in each company, and then study their balance sheets in depth. But throughout, his mind was on his parents' well-being. As a result, though he certainly had the potential for it, he never really made it big in life. He left for work at the Bombay Stock Exchange by 11 a.m. and was back by 5 p.m. My mother hated the stock exchange and thought it was for a bunch of losers. My father would laugh it off. For him, the markets were not as important as his parents. To him, they were his gods. Thinking of him, now I remember the story of Lord Ganesha who circled around his parents, Lord Shiva and Goddess Parvati when asked to cover the three worlds. For Lord Ganesha, his parents were his world.

The other story I remember when I think of my father is of Shravan Kumar, who was the source of support for his blind parents. Shravan took his parents on a pilgrimage across the country, carrying them in two wicker baskets, which he balanced on a rod resting on his shoulder.

My father embodied devotion, sacrifice and love for his parents.

He was an affectionate father as well and I was the apple of his eye. To him, I was what he was to my grandfather and he had towering expectations of me. He had diabetes since the age of eighteen and as I grew up, it would be physically painful to watch his body wither away under the brunt of the disease. In May 1981, my father went to Baroda with my mother, where he felt physically uneasy for the first time. On 12 May 1981, while I was in the USA, I got the news of his death. His passing was peaceful. I, his eldest son, was unable to light his funeral pyre. In all earnestness, I feel that I let my father down in more ways than one.

If my father was a content human being during his lifetime—my mother was a feisty woman with a single-minded focus. Her children had to get the best education and become someone to reckon with.

Her ferocity came from the lack of positive circumstances. Back then, because of the bungalow and my grandfather's legacy, in the eyes of society, we were rich. However, income-wise, we were worse off than the lower middle class.

Just like my father, my mother too had high expectations from me. My father, after all, was only a Senior Cambridge (grade XII) pass. My mother, on the other hand, believed (quite rightly) that education was the key to success. She channelled that passion to her children—even her daughter. She received no support from the family when she insisted that my sister must go to Queen Mary's, rather than the school built by her father-in-law. But my mother held firm. She wanted my sister to learn English and become independent. Her insistence and obstinacy led my sister to gain admission to the best school of the day—and later, to end up with a doctorate in French Literature! My mother was quite as stern with me as she was with my sister.

If I tried to skip school by hiding or feigning illness, my mother would pick me up and physically plant me in class. A couple of times, I had no clothes on! That was her persistence and today, I owe everything to her. My mother's encouragement for education was not limited just to her children but to all the children in the family. My first cousin, who is more like a brother to me, is a successful orthopaedic surgeon and tells stories about how my mother would use every trick in the book, including brute force, to ensure that he went to school. He gives her the credit for his becoming the first doctor in the family. I, too, ended up being the first in the family to go to the United States of America and get an MBA and I only have my mother to thank for the support.

But I was not always as focused as she wanted me to be. I would try to bunk school—the building with which we shared a common wall—by hiding somewhere within the house. My mother would somehow locate me, swoop down upon me like an eagle, pick me up and take me to class!

Back then people used to call me Bhole, short for Bholenath. For her, 'bhola' meant someone dangerously naïve, an idiot, someone with less intellect. This triggered my mother no end. She would insist, 'Become someone in life, or you will perish!' She didn't really know English idioms, but from her, I learned the essence of *necessity is the mother of invention* or, more importantly, *survival of the fittest*. Today, she is all of 100 years old. She continues to stay alone, indomitable and alert. She inspires us all even today. If I have become something akin to a go-getter in life, it is only because my mother taught me not to be anxious about uncharted territories. She would tell me, 'You want to go to America? Then go to America. Make it happen.' These were the words of a woman who was fiercely independent, had seen a lot in life and had allowed nothing to faze her.

Apart from memories of growing up with my parents, I have fond memories of my sister in Shakuntal! Sangeeta was four years older than me and I really loved her. Feisty like my mother, she resembled the legendary actress, Rekha. Growing up, for me, she was the most intelligent and beautiful woman I had ever seen.

Our childhood was filled with togetherness, food, fun, music and laughter, as well as sharing our pain. She was hot-tempered, but the apple of my father's eye. She was an incomparable Kathak dancer and my father encouraged her to pursue her passion. I was younger, but she always made me feel welcome within her circle of friends. In fact, the first movie I ever remember watching in a cinema hall was *Brahmachari*—with Sangeeta and her friends.

Unfortunately, our relationship went downhill in our twenties. Sangeeta was plagued with schizophrenia, a condition which worsened after my father's premature death. She was never diagnosed during childhood, because in our days, mental health was a stigma and knowledge and sensitive awareness of mental health illnesses was practically non-existent. It was only during Sangeeta's last days in hospital—she had been admitted to amputate a leg following a freak accident—that we became close again. She was better then, more lucid and present. I thought I had finally got my sister back—but even then, her days were numbered. She was already prey to galloping diabetes and gangrene.

Sangeeta, my beloved sister, was only fifty-two when she passed away.

As children, my elder sister, my younger brother and I were a trio. In our late twenties, differences of opinion, mistrust, and misunderstanding opened a chasm between the three of us, forcing us to lead parallel lives that never really intersected. Much of this was exacerbated by death and loss and my immaturity as the head of the family post my father's death.

I was twenty-one and my brother was seventeen when our father passed away. I became the head of the family and the business. So I took key decisions. One of them was to send my brother to the US for further studies. The other was to not have a second child, after my daughter was born. I looked out for my brother as if he was my son. He was desperate to become a doctor but his grades were not good enough. I tried my best to secure his admission to Manipal but couldn't help him due to lack of resources. But within a few years, I was doing very well and could afford to send him to the US for further studies to pursue his master's in engineering and subsequently, his MBA.

Once he was back from the US, he joined me in the business. Since I had a firm footing in the trade, I took all the key decisions. Maybe he felt it was my fault that he was doing nothing in the office. Maybe I didn't give him the space to be independent and take his own decisions. For instance, when he thought of our firm, Modern Financial Services, as an integrated stock broking firm on the lines of Merrill Lynch, I didn't allow him the free rein to run it the way he would have liked. I intervened to streamline it and make it successful. Not surprisingly, perhaps, he grew bitter with time and it stained our relationship forever. I don't know what began to go wrong or when. At some point, my own temper flared, thanks to the uncertainties of the business and lack of capital. That's really when our relationship began to break down. I didn't think it would create such an unbridgeable gulf between the two of us. After all, you only show your anger to the people you genuinely care about. But sometimes, even the best intentions are misunderstood. Over the years, my relationship with my brother broke down permanently. To date, he feels that I stifled him and cheated him of the chance to be successful. To date, he no longer speaks to me.

My struggling relationships with my siblings aside, I was deeply influenced by my uncle, Vasantlal Kantilal. Biju Mama, as I fondly called him, was not into the family business. If you asked me, I would have said that he was a literary genius! His understanding of philosophy in general and his knowledge of Jainism in particular was deep. In his lifetime, he wrote and published twenty-four books and had great command over both Gujarati and English.

In fact, the renowned actress Aruna Irani made her stage debut in a Gujarati play that was adapted from one of Biju

Mama's books. He was not interested in making money like the rest of us, but he added great value to our lives as children.

He imparted wisdom to all the children of the family with his stories. The protagonist of his stories was a boy called Batuk—a little person with infinite perseverance. Little Batuk would go through trials and tribulations and come out safe and successful in the end, as he was always right.

Through Batuk, we gained valuable insights: to always look forward, to not be too crushed by an event, and not to become so overjoyed that we lose perspective. Most importantly, we learned the art of giving. Biju mama was a fakir; he gave without considering the consequences. I suppose generosity ran in the family.

He made his own rules, did his own thing and did not care about people's opinions, and I admired that about him. He was a child when he was in the company of children and an adult while discussing philosophy and religion. My favourite childhood moments were those spent with Biju mama. He loved the movies and often took me along with him. After the movie, we would eat sumptuous vegetarian meals at Gaylord Restaurant at Churchgate. He was the best thing in my young life. The days I spent with him were golden moments that I remember with wistful nostalgia even today. I was so happy being around him that I hated to go to school—I simply couldn't bear being apart from him.

Words elude me when it comes to describing his genius and generosity. He found meaning in every word of *Jinagam* which is the sacred book for the Jains, akin to the Upanishads. His interpretation of the nine-line Navkara mantra is referred to even today by sadhus and sadhvis during their *pravachan* (discourse).

My childhood was filled with memories of people who came together to define me in an undeniably unique way.

I was seven when I met a visiting sadhu, who was staying for a while at our home. His name was Tatvananad Vijay Maharaj. There was something about his aura and I was drawn to him immediately. He taught me Jain philosophy in the simplest manner, stating, 'God could have kept the trees, skies, stars to himself. But he gave them to us. He gave us more than what we deserve. The only way to thank him is through sincerity and prayers.'

He taught me how not to be afraid of pain or how not to be angry, giving the example of Bhagwan Mahavir. At one time, when Lord Mahavir was meditating in Samadhi Avastha, someone hammered nails into his ears! Even as Lord Mahavir stoically bore the pain, there was no anger in him.

One day, Sadhu Maharaj noticed how I put aside a plate of food because it was not hot enough. He showed me how frugally the Jain sadhus ate. It was a small plate with everything mixed—dal roti and rice. The food was spartan and cold. Moreover, it was a very small portion. However, all sadhus came together and ate in peace and gratitude. For me, a child who was used to the comforts of life, this was an eye-opener!

My first lesson in right and wrong followed a few years later. In a nook of the bungalow one afternoon, I saw a colony of black ants carrying a dead cockroach. Repulsed by the sight, I sprayed the little convoy with Flit.

Not for a moment did I consider that the carcass of the cockroach might well have been a meal for the ants. Nor did I consider that an action like this was a violation of the tenets of Jainism. My parents, on the other hand, were furious.

I sought guidance from Sadhu Maharaj. He simply said, 'What you have done cannot be undone. But to atone, from now onward start eating less.'

I started the regime of eating once a day from that day onwards. Sometimes I ate just boiled food. There were days I had just boiled water. He taught me about fasting rituals like *ekashana*, *besna*, *ambil* and *upwas*.

I was completely under Sadhu Maharaj's spell. My grandfather noticed and spoke quickly and sharply to my father, 'Do not let your son go to Maharaj Saheb. If you lose him to religion, who will carry our business forward. . .'

* * *

Apart from my key family influencers, our joint family comprised my youngest *kaka* (uncle), his family, and my two *phuis*—my father's sisters. The younger phui was just like my father, a pious and empathetic lady, who loved treating me to scrumptious roadside snacks. I grew up amidst a host of happy, fun-loving cousins. We were all so close that until the sixth or seventh grade, I had no close friends outside my family circle. I didn't feel the need to make friends!

We lived on the principle of sharing is caring. There was no favouritism amongst us children. Everyone helped each other in the time of need. We had seen our father help his family members from time to time. We were shrouded in love and security and I think it was the most holistic upbringing for a child.

I have another distinct memory from my childhood of our Ambassador car (MRY 5727) in which my father would pack all the children of the house and drive to Satkar Udupi Restaurant at Churchgate where we tucked into idlis, dosas and milkshakes. The bill would amount to the princely sum of Rs 4 as there were so many of us. We made family trips to Matheran, and to Radhanpur, in steam-engine trains.

The memories of this joint family continue to be the light of my life. When we saw a photograph, we never said, 'this is me, this is my brother and this is my sister'. We simply referred to it as our family photograph. We were just small dots that made the photograph complete. But all good things must come to an end.

Today, I wish I had spent more time with my grandfather, father and uncle. I wish I had been older when they had been alive. I wish I was allowed to be lost in the company of the Jain sadhus . . .

I would have become a different person, a person I am striving to become today.

2

My Years of Education

There is no end to education. It is not that you read a book, pass an examination, and finish with education. The whole of life from the moment you are born to the moment you die is a process of learning.

—Rumi

1972–1977

'Till today, we have promoted your son. But from now on, he will have to pass on merit. He does not know the 'E' of English, the 'M' of Mathematics, or the 'S' of science. His marks are disgraceful.'

My mother stared speechlessly at the principal.

Thanks to her dogged insistence on education, all the children of our joint family were excelling in academics.

Except for me.

I was her eldest son and her favourite son—and I was way below even the halfway mark of intelligence.

That night, her eyes were red from weeping. She refused to speak to anyone in the family. My father was equally disturbed and told me there was no future without an education. 'I want you to be educated, and not suffer.'

I can't forget that night, even today. It was a milestone. Something shifted in my head and heart that night. I never met Sadhu Maharaj again. Instead, I focused almost single-mindedly on my studies. I never wanted to disappoint my parents that way ever again. The proof, as they say, was in the pudding and after repeatedly standing thirty-eighth in my class, I managed to pull myself up to the eighth position! Suddenly, I was the new star amongst the children of the family. The change in my position was reflected in newfound popularity in school—everyone wanted to be my friend. My luck and circumstances changed and I never really forgot how it made me feel. It was a good feeling and I wanted more of it.

But life had other plans for me.

With every upswing in one's fortunes, there is always a downswing too. I lost both my beloved grandfather and Biju mama within five years of each other. It was a time of intense and painful change at home. Being a joint family, my father and his brothers decided to separate the assets of the family. Though we did not have much, this transition was marred by unnecessary squabbles. For the first time, I started to feel emotionally insecure. Property disputes leave a deep scar in the minds of children. I have seen this in eight out of ten kids, especially the sensitive ones. They begin to respect only money. Sadly, this led to the rise as well as a fall in my life.

As we became financially independent, my father inherited the stockbroking business firm, Kantilal Ishwarlal. At this point, my father was torn between his responsibility towards his children and his mother. His wife, on the other hand, wanted him to focus on the business. Apart from it, we had very few other assets. In her eyes, my father had no other options but to focus on the business. And so it was that at twelve-years-old, I understood what lack of resources and little money meant. I was too young to enjoy ABBA at the time, but in retrospect, their famous song, *Money, Money, Money* made a lot of sense.

> *Money, money, money*
> *Must be funny*
> *In the rich man's world*
> *Money, money, money*
> *Always sunny*
> *In the rich man's world*
> *Aha-ahaaa*
> *All the things I could do*
> *If I had a little money*
> *It is a rich man's world.*

I was not yet in my teens, but I already knew that money signalled power and prestige. If you had money, you could do anything you wanted. That was to become the foundation of my growing years, my life and how I approached the world. I knew now that above all, I had to be successful. Excelling in academics and being financially successful was no longer an aspiration. It was a primal need.

To help me ace mathematics and science, my mother hired a tutor when I was in grade IX. Shyam Mishra was in grade XII, so the age gap was not much.

We shared a wonderful bond. He was my mentor as well as a good friend. He instilled in me a love for Maths and Science. He demystified numbers and formulae for me in the simplest possible way. I had no fear of complex square roots and factors anymore. Our classes were never according to a strict regimen and that was always something I really enjoyed. Often, we'd take

breaks, to simply go and tuck into pav bhaji and kulfi in Khau
Galli at night. Then we'd come back and sit down to solve some
more complex equations and experiments. Shyam taught me a
lot about life as well. The son of an astrologer, he came from a
small town near Baroda. Despite his lack of looks and the lack
of his proficiency in the English language, he was always self-
assured. I learned the skill of being self-confident from him.
He didn't care that he came from nowhere. 'I have come here,'
he would say, 'I am going to study, make money and eventually
have a good life.' I had never seen anyone with such clarity in
what he wanted from life. He was barely eighteen, but he knew
exactly what he wanted. Knowing Shyam only strengthened my
belief in materialism.

By the end of grade X, I was so well prepared that I
watched Amitabh Bachchan's blockbuster *Deewar*, seven days
before my board exams! Mr Bachchan was the youth icon of
our generation. In the dark cinema hall, I was inspired by his
rags-to-riches story and his unconditional love for his mother.

I watched most Amitabh Bachchan movies with my sister
and her friends. Or with Biju mama. My father introduced me
to English westerns. The one film that the entire joint family
watched together was *Sholay*. My father had booked tickets for
the show at the New Excelsior cinema. Sholay was running to
house full shows and we experienced the film from the third
row. I thought to myself—this is how life should be. Romance,
bromance, overcoming challenges, machismo and above all
victory in the end . . . never ever forgetting material success.

I passed grade X with flying colours. I was second in my
school. That I was proud was an understatement, and so were
my parents. While my success should have humbled me, I was
now bursting with grandiosity. In the larger scheme of things,
this was such a small accomplishment . . . but to me and my
family it was larger than life. Everyone started to feed my ego

and I lapped it up. Gradually, I became self-centred and hot-tempered—someone who was waiting for his next validation.

I got admission to the prestigious Sydenham College of Commerce in their first list. Thinking of it as my entry to heaven I was raring to go. At sixteen, I had decided to amass such a fortune that I would retire by fifty.

College was my first taste of freedom and it was a fun place. I made a lot of friends and it included girls as well. Before this, the only girls I knew were from my family. In my very first year, I participated in a college competition in which my humour was appreciated. However, my subsequent stage appearances were a disaster and I was booed off the stage!

I have a distinct memory of a young heir to a well-known textile empire making a dramatic entry into Sydenham in his fancy imported luxury sedans and motorbikes. Every week, it would be a different make. Young girls flocked to him to get a ride in his foreign automobile. And here I was, an obese teenager in baggy pants with a waistline of 44 inches, standing in a queue for a BEST bus. I kept telling myself I was not meant for this. I had to be in that young man's shoes and more. From then on, dreaming became a favourite pastime. I would daydream about all the luxuries wealth could buy. The dream world I created was so vivid and pleasing that stepping out of it to face the mundanities of daily life became a chore.

I started an association in college called The Commerce Workshop. The idea was that students would get acquainted with capital markets and be able to meet the industry leaders. The Workshop was a big hit and I was the one-man-army running it.

Not only did it feed my ego, it more importantly ignited a passion in me. When I took hordes of students to the floor of the Bombay Stock Exchange, my popularity in the community of stock brokers increased manifold. In January 1976, we published our achievement manual, and ironically, my first interview was with the doyen of the Indian textile industry, Kasturbhai Lalbhai, who was the promoter of seven textile mills in Ahmedabad. The idea was to discuss the future of India's textile industry, as it was going through a lean phase. Little did I know back then that I was in conversation with my future wife's grandfather!

During this time, I would visit the stock market with my father. Instead of trading in stocks, our neighbour used to earn brokerage fees from fixed deposits accepted by corporations. People flocked to his office, while ours was empty. I was envious and so I started to learn the dynamics of his business. After all, failure was not an option. From what I had seen in my family, success was a necessity.

Around this time, in 1976–77, many privately held foreign companies like Hindustan Lever and Ingersoll Rand, offered a part of their equity to the public. It was a mandatory provision by the Government of India, spearheaded by our industries minister, George Fernandes. The thinking was that if you wanted to operate in India, part of your holdings would have to be with the public. The issue had to be underwritten and there was what was called underwriters' fees.

My father took me to the then-founder of ICICI— Hasmukhbhai Parekh. He was the uncle of Deepak Parekh. Despite his stature, he was a humble man who had great respect for my grandfather. Hasmukh Bhai Parekh made you feel so comfortable that it was easy to talk to him.

He explained to me that the investment market was ruled by four firms, and the first three gentlemen were referred to as the three 'Indras' of the capital markets:

1) Hemendra Kothari (DSP), later acquired by Merrill Lynch
2) Mahendra Kampani (JM Financial)

3) Bhupendra Dalal (CIFLO Finance)
4) Pradeep Harkisandas (H.L. Finance)

Post this meeting, in my youthful naivete, I promised myself that one day I would break their monopoly. At the same time, I do not know how or why, the idea of going to the United States of America germinated in my mind. As days turned into weeks, I was convinced that the USA was my ticket to success. But I was still a full-time student at Sydenham. I was barely sixteen years old. My father was dead against it. But my mother told me calmly that if I wanted to go to the USA, it was my responsibility to make it happen.

Days later, I stood last in a long serpentine queue waiting for the bus. As I looked ahead, I saw my father standing in the same queue. I felt oddly angered that he should be reduced to taking a bus—at his age and stature in life! Yet at the same time, I kept wondering—*how can I make his life comfortable?* Our family name, Kantilal Ishwarlal, was larger than life. But for us, wealth was limited. We were always anxious of the wealth drying up and if it did, we had no other source of income. After my grandfather died, his sons did not attempt to build on his financial foundation.

I admitted to myself, *'yeh sab khota dikhava hai, Kantilal Ishwarlal this that etc.'* (All this is a façade—this business of Kantilal Ishwarlal, family, prestige etc.) I knew that whatever happened in future, I needed to have money. I wanted to do something fast. When I was in inter-commerce (HSC, grade XII), I came up with a business plan during the Diwali holidays. It was based on intuition and gut feeling, as opposed to the quantitative analysis that today's world is used to. I decided that I would start a fixed deposit brokerage and start underwriting forthcoming issues (public issue on offer of sales). I already knew that I would call it S.S. Kantilal Ishwarlal Securities.

I was extremely aggressive. Stage 1 of the business was to divert clients going to the neighbour's office. I lured them to my office. My modus operandi was disarmingly simple: 'I am offering the same service. I am young. I need to fund money for my education. Please come.'

I went to all the merchant bankers and got my share broking firm business empanelled to be eligible for underwriting. It was an ordeal to keep following up and I am sure many of the people I dealt with then would never have seen such an aggressive person. But my focus was paying off. I was now confident that I would actually be able to go to the US after all—without my father's financial help.

I never stopped working at this time.

If someone wanted to deposit something as little as Rs 2,000, I would go to their house and collect the paperwork—a service that had never been offered to date. Clients were inspired by my focus on going to America and many would ask me to speak to their children about how I had started a business to fund my US aspirations.

Soon enough, the business started doing well. After setting up shop, I barely studied. In fact, in my second year of college, I stopped attending classes. Everyone used to warn me that I would not get the hall ticket to appear for the exams. Our principal, Prof. Abhyankar was strict about discipline and attendance. But I did not care. All I wanted to do was to make money. I did not want to be a CA ticking bank entries. I had to be financially independent and do a job that constantly evolved.

If I simply passed every academic year and moved to the next, I would be okay. At the time, my mind's eye was on the target: the USA. I knew I was on track.

It was around this time that my sister flabbergasted me by saying she wanted to throw a party. My father shocked me even more by agreeing with the idea. Her college friends got LP records from their collection: Elton John, the Bee Gees, Bruce Springsteen, Bob Dylan and Led Zeppelin were all the rage. My father made sure that soft drinks and vegetarian snacks were available for all in copious quantities. Everyone had a great time, but I enjoyed it the most. Back in the 1970s, you went to parties and you came back home by 9 p.m. That night, after the party, my sister invited me out, with a bunch of her friends, to the Taj Mahal hotel. I had never been to a five-star hotel before and as I watched my sister ordering tea and sandwiches, I realized that I was enjoying myself. And yet, I could barely bring myself to eat the delicious food that arrived soon after. I was far too overwhelmed by the grandeur around me. I remember that night very clearly.

We came home by 11 p.m. That is when our father broke the news. Our bungalow was going to be sold. It would be razed and a building would be built. We would get four flats.

I froze. I do not know for how long. It took me a few moments to find my bearings, but the initial shock seemed to go on for an eternity. My knee-jerk reaction was dangerously naïve as well. I was determined to save our bungalow. There was a reason that Amitabh Bachchan's angry young man was my idol. I refused to back down in the face of insurmountable odds. I was going to reclaim this property.

I asked my father if there was anything I could do to save the bungalow. If we could hold on for a few more years, I said, I would work in the USA and send money home.

He stated flatly, 'Shripal, we are in financial difficulty. There is nothing that you can do. For the first time, we met a builder. We will get our four flats with 2,000 square feet each. He will also give us Rs 25 lakh each and interest from it will take care of our expenses.'

I had heard my father recount how heartbroken he had been when they moved out of the sea-facing Eshwar Niwas.

And now for the second time in his life, he was going to have to lose his home.

Going to the US was no longer an aspiration—it was the need of the hour. At the outset, my father was dead against it, but I persisted and so did my mother. After all, business in Bombay had dwindled to nothing. A young man like me had greater prospects in the promised land of the free.

Serendipity intervened when Arvind and Smita Shah from New Jersey came to Bombay for a visit. They both regarded my favourite Biju mama as their guru. My father lost no time broaching the topic saying, 'We do not know anyone in the US. But we want Shripal to go there.' The couple smiled warmly and promised to take great care of me. They told my father not to worry about my well-being in the US as they had helped several families set up in the country. It was done and dusted. After my graduation, I would go to the US and pursue further studies.

This was mid-1976.

A pall of gloom hung over the entire nation. The Emergency was at its height and every young Indian was impassioned with patriotic fervour. I wanted to be a hero. There was a sense of thrill in being part of a pack. I finally had a chance to be like Amitabh Bachchan.

I got hold of an underground organization that gave me access to Amnesty International's papers about human rights abuse in India during the Emergency. I cyclostyled the papers using Sydenham College (incidentally a government college) infrastructure. Of course, the college had no clue about it. Then, at night, I would go to the train shed and place the papers on empty seats of local trains!

My days were long and tiring. In the mornings, I attended to business; the evenings were spent getting the papers cyclostyled. Late at night, I would distribute the papers. My driver, Dattu, became my best friend then and he helped me unknowingly as he had no clue about the contents of the papers.

This went on for five months till on one fateful day—20 March 1977—the police caught me red-handed! I tried to run as fast as I could. However, my consumption of junk food had made me grossly overweight. I was 112 kilos with a 46-inch waistline. I could not run very fast. The police caught up with me at the ticket counter of the railway station. I was mercilessly beaten up. In the police station, I was kicked in the back so violently that there is a spot that hurts even today.

I was incarcerated. Fortunately for me, a day or two later, Prime Minister Mrs Indira Gandhi announced the general elections and at midnight everyone was set free.

I thought my folks would get angry about my night in jail. Instead, I became an instant hero for my father, who gave me his car and driver so that I could campaign for Subramanian Swamy and Jaswant Rajda, both from the newly formed Janata Party. I made a group of five like-minded college friends. Ah! The thrill of campaigning! Shouting in the middle of the road at the top of your voice, passersby staring at you at the signal, never having to pay for your chai and batata wada. It was exhausting but worth it. Hard work paid off and my photograph appeared with Ratansinh Rajda, who later became an MP, in the newspapers.

At that time, the Janata Party was a fledgling party. The bubble of patriotism was growing bigger and bigger by the day. And as bubbles usually do, they burst sooner than later. The new government fell within eighteen months of its formation.

1977 was a definitive year for India, not only politically but financially as well. The public issue of Reliance Industries Limited was entering the market. Through my aunt's son, who knew Anil Ambani very well, I had the good fortune of meeting the great Dhirubhai Ambani. That was a time when meeting him was relatively easy.

I still remember what he said: 'Everyone makes besan. I make fried bondas. Thus, my yield is higher than the others.' That was his way of explaining the concept of value addition—while everyone else sold yarn, he sold the finished product—polyester.

Dhirubhai Ambani was the second industrialist I met after Kasturbhai Lalbhai. At that time, he had the vision that one day he would go into all aspects of backward integration. During the meeting, he got several calls from the higher echelons of the government, and I was impressed by the way he spoke. His pidgin English paled in comparison to his focus, crystal-clear thinking, and over-arching vision. He was ambitious, knew exactly where he was going, and I perceived his determination to succeed.

Before I left the meeting, Mr Ambani asked me about my bank balance. I flatly stated I had Rs 4,00,000 that I had made from my business and I was going to use it for my American dream. He said, 'Instead, buy Reliance for 4 lakh, lock it in your vault, and open it only if there is a financial emergency.'

Now, for context, you must note that during those days, the foundations of the bull market in India were just about getting laid. You first bought into IPOs of foreign and national companies at throwaway prices, then you bought companies like Reliance (the pricing of the equities issued by the company was determined by an archaic formula employed by the Controller of Capital Issues which ensured the price of issuance was very low).

Many people who invested in this manner back then are now billionaires today. Many people who had then invested in stocks of Hindustan Lever, Ingersoll Rand, Reliance, Larsen and Toubro—even in small quantities are billionaires without doing much other than just sticking to their investments.

I remember one such individual who had so much faith in Century Textiles that he bought the scrip with whatever savings he had. He did this till 2007–2008, by which time he had a million shares of Century Textiles. After the meeting, I was conflicted. Should I be investing in shares? Should I forget my American dream and focus on multiplying my wealth through investments? Instead, I chose the hard way. After all, I was the 'enthu-cutlet' who wanted to create wealth through business creation, toil and perspiration.

Dhirubhai Ambani had created wealth out of nothing. I thought to myself, if he can do it, so can I. I could set up and build a company after my American dream, which will not only make me rich but others as well.

I made up my mind. I would not invest in stocks. I would only invest in the businesses that I created and so, deliberately and a tad arrogantly, I chose to ignore the foundation of the bull market.

Investing in other people's companies, banking on the ability of promoters, and multiplying capital did not excite me. I was all for the hard work that went into building a business and benefitting from my inspiration, ideas, and perspiration, as opposed to capital employment.

3

Going to the USA

My soul is from elsewhere,

I am sure of that
I intend to end up there.

—Rumi

May 1979

The die was cast. Mine was a conscious decision to pursue the American Dream. Why should I rely on money made by other people's efforts? I wanted to own a business, not just some minor stocks in that business. But I had no clue how this would pan out. In those days, getting a student visa was challenging. It was worse because I resisted taking the TOEFL and GMAT (exams that judged English and Math proficiency respectively) which were mandatory to get the I-20 forms for college application. I am not sure if I was being lazy or if it was the fear of getting poor grades. I was so focused on making money to fund my trip to the US that I did not have the time for 'petty exams'.

In December 1978, I wrote to six US institutions stating that I was a victim of human rights violations during the Emergency. I was jailed during the Emergency, I wrote plaintively (I did not specify the period!). This bit of playing the victim card was more about creating a deliberate emotional impact on the Americans, who are well known as the greatest advocates of human rights. This, I thought, was the best way to get the visa. After all, I did not have any meaningful assets to show the US authorities and prove that I intended to return. We had sold our bungalow, got a flat and each head of the family had received Rs 25 lakh. From the interest of the surplus generated, my father used to take care of our expenses. So there was not much to show. To the authorities, it would mean I had no reason to return to India.

Business failure, coupled with diabetes is a lethal combination. My father was under immense stress and was gradually withdrawing from the business. He had high expectations that I would succeed in life. He was impressed by the success of SSKY, my small investment consultancy services and he was proud of my extracurricular activities in college like the Commerce Workshop.

In January, I got a letter from two institutions. I remember that it was a Friday. My father was pacing up and down, waiting for me. I had gone to meet a client. As soon as I returned to the office, my father told me about the two mails. I said he must open them. My father asked me to chant three Navkar Mantras (the most important spiritual mantras in Jainism). After reciting the mantras, I reached out for the envelope from NYSE, least bothered about the second envelope which was from Disney.

I remember the entire office staff of six people clustering around my father and me. I asked my father to read the letter out loud. There was rejoicing in that office after a very long time. The staff was as chuffed as my father. My heart was in the New York Stock Exchange! And thus, the second letter from Walt Disney was, in effect, inconsequential.

The NYSE did not have a training programme, but I was assured by Mr Robert Bishop, senior vice president of NYSE, that he would create a special programme after meeting me and understanding my goals.

It was decided that I would go in April or May 1979. Now, I had to send a letter confirming my acceptance.

In those days, we did not have a typewriter in the office. We would go to a small shop down the road where typists from Kerala typed on electronic typewriters. They usually took large assignments from lawyers. However, with me, they made an exception. After all, I had a letter from the prestigious NYSE! I got my letter typed and had a celebratory drink! I glugged two chilled glasses of nimbu paani from a family-run lemonade stall that exists even today! Then I went to the office, took my father's signature, rushed to the General Post Office in a taxi, and posted my acceptance letter via registered post.

With the NYSE letter, I had killed two birds with one stone. Now, getting a visa would be a cakewalk, and I would be trained in the biggest stock exchange in the world!

Just before going to the US, I took a solo trip to Goa. My entire family thought I was going there for the 'babes'. My reason was different. I grew up in a joint family. I wanted to know if I could live alone in the company of people who ate meat, smoked, and consumed alcohol and banned substances, and yet be a teetotaller.

The trip to Goa was an eye-opener in many ways. It was my first time on an airplane. The shacks on Calangute beach were worse than the ones in the dharmshalas of religious towns. I met a lot of people—hippies—as we call them now. Drugs were cheap and available in copious quantities. Even in those days, alcohol flowed like water in Goa.

The foreign tourists spent most of their money on these two vices, without thinking about tomorrow. They would work in their country for four to five months, book the cheapest flights and stay in shacks for a couple of months or more. I saw Goa as the vice capital of India, and it strengthened my conviction that drugs, alcohol and meat were not for me. In fact, I was disgusted by drugs and alcohol. I saw many locals and foreigners getting wasted by the excess. I succeeded in remaining clean and was very proud of myself.

I also made sure to enjoy myself. I stayed in shacks and spoke with tourists. Almost all of them were white, and I wondered what brought them to India. Soon I realized that most were intrigued by a mystical India. There were two popular destinations everyone visited: Goa, known for its Portuguese culture and beaches, and Varanasi, recognized as the spiritual hub of India. Incidentally, ganja/marijuana was freely available in both places. They were enchanted by the fact that ganja was part of our tradition and that even some followers of our gods and goddesses smoked it. Everyone, even back then, talked about meditation. And even though I was Indian, meditation still felt like an alien concept.

After I returned, my best friend from college suggested a trip to our ancestral hometown of Radhanpur, as well as to the holy pilgrimage sites of Palitana and Sankeshwar. In the temples, I noticed a distinct difference in how I prayed compared to my friend. My prayers felt superficial; I was not seeking wisdom and strength but was instead consumed by a desire for fleeting things, my mind racing like a drunken monkey. In contrast, my friend's prayers were profound and meditative, and the stillness of his mind was remarkable. After praying, he radiated a beatific glow, and his aura seemed to brighten. However, I was so enchanted by the prospect of going to the US that none of this mattered to me at the time.

The clock was ticking towards D-Day. My preparations were in full swing. There was a popular class called Nazareth Public Speaking, run by a husband-wife team. I took a short course in public speaking and communication and came first in the class.

I did not know how to wear a tie. I got three double-breasted suits crafted by Raymond. But nothing would hide my expanding waistline, as I was invited by friends and family for innumerable lunches and dinners. My parents were insecure and anxious about my departure. They were frequently on calls with Arvind and Smita in New Jersey. Back in the late seventies, people made trunk calls. International calls were a nightmare! Many a time, the operator was a good Samaritan who stepped in to relay what my parents said to Arvind and Smita as their voices were inaudible. She would then communicate Arvind and Smita's response back to my parents. And mind you, these international 'trunk calls' were very expensive.

Finally, it was time to leave. My flight was at 5.30 a.m. A person who had never eaten potato, onion, garlic, or anything that grew under the soil, who did not have a clue about what pizza or French fries were, was making his first-ever international trip to America with a determination to settle there. I was the first in my family to travel overseas.

My obsession with the US stemmed from the stories I had heard. Even people in menial jobs owned cars and homes. I told myself that if I was educated and hardworking, there would be no stopping me. The rat race would be much shorter. Education is a continuous process, and when technology and time overtake you, age is not a barrier to attending college in the US.

I took with me two lessons from my parents:

- Necessity is the mother of invention: If you are determined, despite the obstacles, you will surely make it happen.
- Never expect the expected: The expected never happens. Today, I'm sixty-five-years-old and finally learning the essence of these words.

These two diktats were etched in my ambitious heart through life, giving me strength to fight adversities.

Back in 1979, there was no concept of terror threats and visitors could get an entry ticket to the terrace of the airport to bid farewell to their loved ones. As I walked towards the bus that would drive me to my plane, I heard my father shout my name just once – *Shripal!*

The word 'Shripal' echoes even today and I get goosebumps. It was a cry filled with unconditional love, and concern for me. Maybe he knew that it was the last shout out to me from Indian soil.

Tears rolled down my cheeks, refusing to stop. That twenty-four-hour-journey was highly emotional. I could not eat anything on the flight. For the very first time, I also became conscious of my weight. I asked for water, but I could barely sip it. This was compounded by the biggest fear—what if I could not adjust to the new life in an alien country? The truth always hits you at the last moment. What if I failed? What if I did not like it there? It is good to have dreams, but was I ready to face the consequences of the failure of the sky-high expectations I had set for myself and that my family set had for me?

Gaping into a black hole with no answers, I landed at JFK airport in New York at 2 p.m.

There was a long queue at immigration. And now I was anxious about the next moment. Would they stamp my entry? Rejections were common at airports, and I had known of people who had been deported. What would they ask me?

An African–American immigration officer with a shrill voice checked my passport. She asked me what the purpose of my visit was. I told her how we (my family) were the largest stockbroking firm in India. I was not far from the truth and should have simply added 'once upon a time'. Moreover, I added that I had come to learn the systems at the New York Stock Exchange and implement them locally. She bellowed a 'wow' and put the stamp on my passport. I was relieved.

It took me an hour to find my bags. Finally, I went out. Arvind and Smita were waiting for me. During those days, Smita's parents were also in New Jersey. They were from a small town in Gujarat. Arvind had an old Chevrolet and we drove down to the famous New Jersey Turnpike and took exit 9 to reach their residence. Arvind and Smita lived in an upper-middle-class New Jersey neighbourhood. They had a massive house, great cars and their children spoke in a thick American accent. All of Arvind's friends in the neighbourhood had rags-to-riches stories. There was a doctor from Bombay who was distantly related to us. He was a successful paediatrician in New Jersey. In Bombay, he lived in a pint-sized one-bedroom-apartment. In New Jersey, he lived in a seven BHK in an area that was less than ten kilometres away from the prestigious Ivy League Princeton University. I thought that America was a place where everyone succeeded. Most Indians had wealth beyond their wildest dreams.

It was Arvind and Smita who explained the layout of New York to me. I was already disappointed by Brooklyn and Queens. Only when we entered Manhattan did I sit up with some interest. The tall buildings were representative of my sky-high hopes from life. The traffic was buzzing with fancy cars. Would I ever own one of those vehicles that could support my high-speed desire? The quality and size of the roads made me go 'wow!' so many times. Yes, there was traffic, but it was constantly moving. All of these discoveries inspired me to hope that one day I could move to the area of my choice—Manhattan. Arvind and Smita truly treated me like a son. On my part, I helped with the chores as much as I could. From the third day onwards, I mowed their lawns. I would pick up milk and other groceries from the neighbouring WAWA store. It was a 24/7 store—the older version of a contemporary 7/11. I would pluck fresh peaches from the trees. I struggled with the vacuum cleaner. Since I had never seen one before, it took me quite a while to get adjusted to it. Its elongated wire would wind around the table, and I was scared that something would fall.

During the day, I explained my plan. In tandem with my training at NYSE, I wanted to apply for an MBA programme. But on the very first weekend, I had a fall on the steps of their house. The pain was so excruciating that in the night I cried myself to sleep, thinking of my mother.

The next day, the couple suggested I take a dip in their swimming pool. It was the first time I had seen a pool in a house. The sheer joy of being in the pool, even if I did not know how to swim, was something I will never forget.

Arvind and Smita had helped over fifty families settle in the US and create meaningful lives for themselves. Arvind came from a humble background. Highly spiritual from a young age and blessed by my Biju mama's teaching, he would always step in if someone needed genuine help. They were not flamboyant at all.

But many of their friends were. One friend would probably have lived in a three BHK back in India. But in New Jersey, he had a swimming pool with his mansion. Flowers bloomed in his garden while he was discussing the next family holiday on a cruise ship. Back then, I had no idea what a cruise ship meant. I saw for the first time Indian professionals planning vacations for a year in advance to foreign countries and exotic haunts that I had never heard of.

The other friend was a textile merchant. He was married to a white American woman and thus had quick access to the coveted Green Card. The opulence of the US whetted the materialistic instinct in me. I had razor-sharp focus. 'I will do anything and everything—including marrying a Green Card holder for visa purposes,' I said to myself that Sunday night. I had arrived on Friday. I had packed in a lot in just three days!

On Monday at 2 p.m., was my first interview with Robert Bishop, senior vice president, New York Stock Exchange, in his office at 11, Water Street. Smita dropped me off at the bus station and said that since she was busy in the evening, I should walk back home.

I nodded like a cow, but frankly, I did not give a damn as I was nervous about meeting a very senior official of the New York Stock Exchange. I boarded the bus that took me to Times Square. It was vast, colourful and confusing. The help desk at Times Square Bus Station was occupied by an aged African–American gentleman and he saw how lost and helpless I was.

He then took out the map of New York and explained the layout of the entire city. That is when I realized I was in mid-town and had to go downtown! And that the tube station was right in Times Square. Those days, it used to cost 50 cents to buy a token . . . and lo and behold, I was on my first subway trip. New York was not the crime-free city that it is now. The crime statistics were high, and every five seconds, my hand would reach into my coat to check if my wallet was still there.

I took a seat. Soon, I was cornered by two of the weirdest men I had ever seen. One guy was bleeding from his scalp and was constantly talking to himself. The second guy was constantly badgering me for a quarter of a dollar. I froze as I did not know how to react. At that time, I was so naïve that I thought I was going to be killed. That is when I realized that until then, I had lived such a sheltered life that I now felt like Simba released from a zoo into the most dangerous jungle.

Finally, Water Street Station arrived. I alighted and asked a fifty-plus man, eating a pretzel, where 11, Water Street was. He walked me to the street and said, 'Buddy, here you go. Go to the 15th floor.' Incidentally, he too, worked at the NYSE.

I remembered a line I had learned from my Nazareth Public Speaking classes: 'Words are insufficient to express my gratitude.' Saying this, I bowed to him. He smiled and walked away.

I looked around. The entire street was filled with men in crisp suits and ties. Looking at their determined stride gave me a high. I knew I was in the right place.

Wall Street was so different from Dalal Street—sophisticated with its ambitious, well-dressed men, fancy cars and open garages.

People on Dalal Street wore dhotis. The ring was not air-conditioned. The smell of human sweat, sprinkles of paan spit, and farts clogged the air. I distinctly remember one guy who used to run the illegal options trade on Dalal Street. His legs would bleed because of the incessant scratching. It was a grotesque sight. I wanted desperately to be a Wall Street man in contrast.

I took the elevator to the 15th floor. The size of the lift was baffling and its speed terrifying (it was my very first trip in an automatic elevator). *What if the lift stops,* I thought to myself, *who would help me?* I breathed a sigh of relief when the door opened.

At the reception, I asked for Bob Bishop's office. A charming lady in her mid-fifties came into view. She smiled warmly at me, before hugging me. I returned the gesture awkwardly. It was, after all, the first time that I had been hugged by a woman outside my family. Then I was taken into Bob's room. Bob Bishop was a tall man, with a shock of white hair and silver-rimmed spectacles. He was extremely soft-spoken. I don't know if you believe in phenomena like a past-life connection, but I was instantly at ease in his presence. He told me that he was interested in having me on board, because of my family's background on Dalal Street, and because he loved the culture of the East. His eldest son's wife was Korean. Then, out of the blue, he invited me to his home for dinner with his family. On Friday, he said, we could meet at the office and take the train back to his residence. I was stumped! Very few businessmen in America invite you to have dinner with their family.

'If you think New York City is fast, then let me tell you, the New York Stock Exchange is ten times faster!' he told me, laughing in the same breath. He explained that as the NYSE was often slow to react, other liberal exchanges had started and were vying to compete with NYSE businesses. Bob helped me understand the listing criteria as well. How were new companies evaluated? How were trading patterns studied to see if any fraud was underway? But he also said something I did not quite understand. He said that as more intelligent people came to the Exchange, they would create such products that would have an impact on the entire nation. I did not understand what he was talking about back in 1979 as I knew only basic terms like shares, bonds and fixed deposits. That was what I had been exposed to till that day . . . until catastrophe struck thirty years later, with the Lehmann crisis in 2008. When it happened, I thought of Bob Bishop and the words he had spoken in 1979.

At the end of the meeting, Bob said that I had to start the following Monday and train for eight weeks in a row. He made it a point to understand what exactly I was looking for

and promised me a schedule the next day that would provide
training in a mid-size brokerage house and all departments
of NYSE.

At nineteen, all this was new to me. I could not wait to start!

* * *

The first thing I did after the meeting was to place a collect
call (in which the receiver would pay for the call) to my father
in India, even though it was late at night there. I repeated my
conversation with Bob word for word, throwing in all the terms
I knew now—*insider trading, patterns, listing criteria*. My father
listened proudly. His pride was so evident that from that day
onwards, I made up my mind that whatever happened in life, I
would first tell my parents.

After the call, I went to the pizzeria and like a fool, asked
for a vegetarian pizza. I did not even know what a pizza was.
Hungry with excitement, I gorged on seven slices of margherita
pizza and washed it down with a tall bottle of Coke to celebrate
this new turn my life had taken.

4

Life in America

When sorrow comes, be kind to it

For God has placed a pearl in sorrow's hand.

—Rumi

May 1979–May 1981

The dinner with my new mentor and his family at their home was on Friday evening. I used the time from Monday to Thursday to acquaint myself with the world's major financial, commercial and cultural city.

New York was a city like no other. It pulsated, quite literally, with ambition, glamour and glitz. I soaked it all in that week, as I walked through the city—around landmarks like the Empire State Building, the Statue of Liberty, Central Park, the mass of skyscrapers downtown, the neon-lit malls with their array of brands. I knew instinctively that I wanted to be a part of this some day. This was where I wanted to live. The thought kept running through my head as I walked through Times Square.

Did you know that Times Square is named after the *New York Times*, which moved its office there in 1904? Until then, it had been called Longacre Square. But when I was wandering around there, in the late 1970s, Times Square was the epicentre of crime and vice in New York City. Theatres showed porn films; there were stage shows with live sex and for a quarter (25 cents), you could touch the private parts of a woman's body. The smell of marijuana on the streets was appalling. People spewed expletives and alcoholics guzzled from bottles held in brown paper bags. There were smoke clouds from the subway and chimneys, and graffiti was everywhere I looked. In those two days, I discovered Manhattan in its true essence. It had a beautiful and aspirational side to it, as well as a bestial one that had to be avoided at any cost.

I remember that when Friday finally came around, I was a bundle of excitement and nerves. Until now, I had never had a meal with high-profile professionals. Back home, we would look at the NYSE with reverence—and now, one of their seniors had taken a personal interest in me and had called me for dinner. I was over the moon!

Bob Bishop introduced me to his family—his wife, his oldest son who was thirty-one, and daughter-in-law, and their younger kids—an eighteen-year-old daughter, and a twelve-year-old son.

I was a mess at the dinner table. I did not know how to eat spaghetti with a fork and spoon or how to cut a piece of potato using a fork and knife! My potato ricocheted from the plate to the table. However, Bob and his family did not flinch and ignored the faux pas, continuing the conversation as though nothing had happened.

I was more grateful for that generosity than they would ever know. After the lights and smoke of Times Square and the glitz of the city outside, I finally felt as though I was home.

After dinner, Bob explained the training programme to me and gave me a detailed rundown of my schedule for the next two months. I was supposed to go to the various departments of the New York Stock Exchange and study how it functioned. I told him that it was a dream come true for me. What I did *not* tell him was that I planned on staying in the US for more than the scheduled eight weeks. My dreams were bigger—I wanted to study further and settle in the USA.

Before I left, I thanked Bob and his family for their time and consideration. I had a spring in my step and a rumble in my tummy. I had barely eaten after all! At the first McDonald's on the way to the station, I stuffed my face with two large packets of French fries, washing the greasy meal down with a large Coke.

* * *

On Monday morning, I put on my best suit and tie. The start of a new chapter in my life. I was introduced to all the heads of departments, which must have been protocol, but for me, it felt as though I was a VIP. I met Bob's peers, many of whom took a shine to my innocence. I was taken to classy restaurants by the seniors, though when I was with the junior staff, we opted for pizza.

During my training, on 28th–32nd Street on Lexington Avenue, I discovered a host of Indian restaurants, ranging from cheap street food to stylish diners. There were also Chinese options that offered vegetarian food. So, I had no problem finding vegetarian meals in the USA. I had no urge whatsoever to experiment—with meat, alcohol or drugs. I was very happy with what life was offering.

I was enjoying my staple—pizzas and French fries.

Whenever I got off the train at 42nd Street, Times Square, I would have French Fries. I was so regular that the man behind the counter would see me and say, 'French fries, right?'

I felt at home in America and was most impressed by the way they spoke respectfully even to strangers. For the first time, I was beginning to understand the meaning of the dignity of labour. America taught me that you can overcome anything, if you are hardworking and polite.

I put that into practice in earnest—and still do. It has stood me in good stead across the world in good and bad times.

As weeks flew past, I thought I had overstayed my welcome with Arvind and Smita. I needed to be independent. So I decided to stay at the YMCA for two days, at $3 per night. But the place was stinking and packed to the brim with the kind of people I couldn't bring myself to live with, much less associate with. My upbringing had been a fairly sheltered one, now that I look back. To me, anyone with a tattoo was a pot-smoking hippie and must be avoided at all costs. That wasn't the case at work, of course, which was a clean, sterile environment, peopled with ambitious and polished men. While I figured out how the world of the New York Stock Exchange worked, I couldn't help thinking that it was a far cry from the humid and unsophisticated (in those days!) Dalal Street.

In the early 1980s, a big petroleum company's stocks nosedived, seemingly for no reason. Investigation into the matter revealed that it had been shorted by many traders. It was my opinion that this stock would eventually go through the roof because of the NYSE's actions, compelling short-sellers to cover their positions. In my naivete, I told my relatives to buy that stock. If I had done that today, I would be behind bars on charges of insider trading! But my relatives were, of course, so impressed by my knowledge that they asked me to manage a fund for them, once I had settled in school.

By the time my training was over, I had learned about every department of the New York Stock Exchange. After that, I was assigned to the back office of a mid-size brokerage firm. It was so systematically organized, that saying I was impressed is an understatement. I would describe my experiences to my father who in turn boasted to family, friends and fellow brokers that his son had become an expert on the New York Stock Exchange! Little did he know that it took ages to gain expertise on any exchange, leave alone the New York Stock Exchange.

But the clock was ticking. I had to get admission to a college for my master's degree. For the next fifteen days, I devoted myself to finding a college. New York University was my first love. I also went to Pace University and St John's University to see if I could gain admission there. But without a GMAT score, they would not admit me. I tried to convince them to take me, based on my business experience. I had genuinely made a breakthrough and created a business of my own, but no one wanted to acknowledge that I had been trained at the New York Stock Exchange! But it seemed that what I thought was amazing wasn't everyone else's view. The universities I was applying to wanted more—a GMAT and TOEFL score in addition to my work experience and internship.

It was now that serendipity stepped in. One of our neighbours from Bombay arrived with bags packed with theplas and dhoklas that my mother had sent for me. As we sat and sipped the tea and ate the theplas, he listened to my problems. At the end of my rant, he told me that my best hope, given my credentials, was Wagner College in Staten Island.

I didn't waste a moment. I submitted my credentials and forms to Wagner College. It wasn't the best, but it was reasonably well-respected. Moreover they asked me just one question—'will you be able to pay your fees?'

I nodded vigorously and was handed an I-20 form. (An I-20 form is filed with the New York Immigration authorities to get a student visa). I would now need to convert my B-1/B-2 visa to a F-1 (student visa). Armed with an I-20 form, I had now climbed yet another rung of the ladder.

Now, I had to procure the visa. It was easier said than done. I took a ferry from Staten Island to Water Street. Meeting Bob was important for this. In his office, I was nearly in tears with anxiety. His secretary saw my distress and asked me immediately if I was all right. To me, it was just another sign that in America, the people were so much different from how they were in India.

I told the secretary that I had worked hard to finally get myself admitted to a school. 'Will you be kind enough and give me five minutes with Mr Bishop?' The kind secretary replied, 'He is in a meeting. He will be free at 2 p.m.'

Around 2.15 p.m. I was called in. That hour-long wait felt like a lifetime. Bob was to the point. 'What can I do for you?'

'Sir,' I began nervously, 'I have learned so much from you in a few months—and my undergraduate courses, starting my business, or BSE—all combined cannot match up to what I learned from you in four months. I learned to view an organization holistically. I learned to understand the strengths and weaknesses of an organization and the importance of good leaders and workers. But what would be truly wonderful, sir, would be if I could study here.' I was gaining confidence as I rattled on and he listened patiently. 'I want to be able to broaden my horizons and increase my opportunities. My only problem is that I am on a tourist visa. I can go back to India and reapply from there—but what would be faster would be if I could get a letter of recommendation from you, addressed to the immigration authorities. That way, I could convert my visa from a B1–B2 to an F-1, without having to leave for India.'

Twenty minutes later, Bob's signature flashed across the left corner of my letter of recommendation. I was so grateful! I went immediately to the immigration authorities and I handed in my application.

I informed Arvind and Smita about my admission to Wagner College and application for a student visa. Term began in September. Smita helped me make a list of things I would need in college and we got down to shopping. My waistline had whittled down to 40 inches and I had to acquire a new wardrobe for fall and winter.

Soon I was running out of money. I thought my father had been paying out of the savings I had made from the SSKI business. Sometimes, he would tell me to 'take the money from Smita, and I'll pay her back'. I thought nothing of it in the way that young people do. Little did I know that he was under immense financial strain. One of his sub-broker clients had lost a lot of money. When bad luck shrouds a business, its domino effect is striking. My father, unknown to me, had lost not only his business but also the money he had got from the sale of our bungalow.

I had no idea. My father, who knew all about my attempts to start afresh in America, didn't want to burden me with worries. He knew that had I known, I would have given everything up to come back home. I adored my parents, and I would never have let them experience a moment's unease. As it was, it was only when my father told me to take on a day job to pay my fees that I realized that something was wrong.

I remember that it was 2 September when I began college. There was a buzz of youthful enthusiasm on campus. But I was restless.

That night was one of the gloomiest nights of my life. I was homesick. I missed my parents dearly. Something wasn't right at home. I knew it in my gut. I remember walking aimlessly around the campus. The sun had set earlier than usual. I had only seen spring and the summer in America so far. But now, fall was slowly making its way into the air. Music was blaring from one of the dorm halls. Unlike other students who enjoyed the bonhomie, I was all by myself. The pounding drum beats increased my anxiety. I felt thoroughly out of place that night.

The next twelve months were a struggle—emotionally, financially as well as academically. But I decided to grit my teeth and push on. It was, I reasoned to myself, what my father would want me to do. From day one, I took up odd jobs.

I was in a hurry. Much against the wishes of my advisor, I took eighteen credits and six credits (three credits each for my thesis) that spread over two semesters. Generally, students averaged nine–twelve credits. However, I intended to finish my thesis and MBA in two semesters. The thesis was going to be a comparison between the New York Stock Exchange and the Bombay Stock Exchange. I explained to my advisor that I was in a rush, because of financial problems back home. I didn't know how close to the truth I was with that unconscious lie. But if a lie could help me accelerate my studies, so be it. I worked to clear the falling autumn leaves off the campus lawns, and as an assistant at the library. At that time the minimum wage was less than $3 per hour. However, when I would receive my paycheque, it felt like a fortune.

I still was in touch with my father, telling him everything I was doing and the money I was making. He was delighted, though he didn't mention a word about his financial distress. Looking back now, I can see both of us disguising our truths from one another. He was sure I would revive the failing business when I was done with my time in America. I didn't tell him that I had no intention of leaving the United States. Nor did I tell him that struggling to make tuition was challenging, to say the least. I was doing more than two jobs at one point: shovelling snow, working as a salesperson in an Indian store on Lexington Avenue, waiting tables, and teaching economics and accounting to undergrad students who needed special attention. Hell, I was even a manager at McDonald's on the weekends!

Then, someone told me that being a security guard on weekends paid well. So after classes on Friday nights, I would report to the Holiday Inn as a security guard on duty. My job entailed climbing fourteen floors three times a night to do my rounds. It was exhausting, but I made $120–140 in one night! It was fun. I was young, so I never felt physical exhaustion. Moreover, it helped me lose unwanted inches from my waist. But there were times when it was difficult to see the bright side. I remember one day in December when I was walking back to college from the Holiday Inn. We had to climb a huge, steep slope to go to the dormitory. Even at nineteen, I had to pause several times to climb up that slope. That cold December morning, I felt my socks getting drenched. I looked down to see that the soles of my shoes had worn out, and snow was seeping through them. I did not have money to buy shoes.

The next day, I went to my regular McDonalds and said, 'I have not come as a customer. Do you have a job for me? I am an MBA student and would like to work here on weekends.' They nodded and handed me a mop. I was exhausted from juggling so many jobs. But there was no choice. I needed a pair of shoes.

With all jobs combined, I made $1000 a month. It was barely enough to pay for my expenses, including college fees. At one point I worked as a coolie for Fashion Street. Clothes were shipped from India, and I executed the offload, packaging, and dispatch to places like JC Penny and the warehouses of other international brands.

Despite the exhaustion from multiple jobs, I did not reduce credits or work. But I started taking uppers—tablets to keep me awake so that I could study. Though the fatigue from doing multiple odd jobs pulled me down physically, I did not want my grades to tumble. I knew my college was not the best and if I got anything less than 4.0, Summa Cum Laude, no one would even recognize me or the efforts I had put in.

Back home the impression was that I was having a great time and I had a lot of girlfriends. I let them think what they wanted. I did not want to let anyone know about the struggle to make ends meet.

As far as people on the campus were concerned, I was treated with great respect by the white and African–American students. Surprisingly, it was the Indian community on the sixth floor of the Wagner College dormitory that made my life hell. They were largely from South Indian states like Andhra Pradesh, Tamil Nadu, Hyderabad and Kerala. There was one boy from Malaysia, but he too had South Indian roots. For some reason, I was singled out. You see, they all thought I was a prudish rich Bombay boy. Indeed, I never felt the need to indulge in alcohol or drugs. But it is not true that I was rich. That was the irony of my life: folks on the NY Stock Exchange thought I was from a rich family as did my professors. My fellow students thought I was a rich kid studying in the US. As a result, I often got the cold shoulder. If I wanted to leave, they would lock the door. There wasn't a moment when they were not stoned, and when they were stoned, they would verbally abuse me. As a victim of bullying, I can only say that the memories are etched in your heart.

My only solace was the occasional clubbing. But there, too, I did not fit in—I did not know how to dance. After some time, even that stopped, and I focused only on work and studies. And guess what? At the end of my postgraduate degree, I scored a 4.0 average which was the highest one could get! I won the Wall Street Journal Award for Excellence in Management

Studies. I got an A+ on my thesis. My father was extremely proud of me, and with equal pride, I invited my parents to come for my graduation ceremony.

It was at this point that I began to realize, with even greater clarity, that something was not right at home. For one, I heard that my mother had indicated to the folks at home that Shripal had sent tickets for them to fly out to the United States. That wasn't true, of course. I could barely take care of myself, let alone my parents. When they finally arrived, I began to grow more suspicious and bewildered. My parents weren't telling me something and it was so obvious that it created a chasm between us. On a trip to Florida, I could see that they weren't enjoying themselves. The elephant in the room made us so awkward around each other that I could hardly bear it. Still, I kept quiet— until finally, I think my father's tolerance wore thin too. One day, he blurted out bluntly, 'Shripal, we have no money.'

I froze. His words shattered my world. Then, in a knee-jerk reaction that I can't quite explain even in retrospect, I blurted out that I would start making money after a year. With a mix of bravado and fear, I said that soon my father could retire and everything would be fine, I insisted. But it was the first time that I felt a different kind of pressure. Looking after myself was one thing—feeling the burden of looking after *everything* to do with my home and parents was something else entirely. I forgot that this was a moment of celebration. How could I remember it when my parents were quite literally staring into an abyss? What good was I to them, if I couldn't help them? But *how* could I help them? Thoughts were whirling in my head. I tried to be as fine as I could be under the circumstances, but I was a bad actor. I lost my temper several times with them, snapping at them for nothing.

Looking back, I feel bad about how I reacted then. But I was twenty-one-years-old. My family still didn't know the hardships I had had to endure to get where I was. Somewhere under the anxiety, resentment seethed. Days later, we bade each other awkward goodbyes at the airport. It was the last time I would see my father.

I wish now that our time in America was different.

I started hunting for jobs. Job vacancies were listed in the *Wall Street Journal* and the *New York Times*. I read both every day and kept an eye out for job prospects. Most available jobs were in the insurance sector, but I was not keen on a career in insurance sales.

I went for interviews every day, but not having a work visa, doors were shut on me.

Yet again, serendipity smiled upon me.

One day, I met someone who worked for a brokerage firm called Burt Reynolds. He was much older and I treated him like a father figure. Soon enough, he hired me to work at the Burt Reynolds office in East Orange.

My work wasn't particularly challenging. It involved perusing the Yellow Pages—the telephone directory in those days—and cold-calling prospective clients stating, 'I am Paul Morakhia. I work for Burt Reynolds. Can I please come in and explain the products and schemes we have?'

Not surprisingly, my heart was not in it—and it showed. I barely had three or four clients. After the drive and hustle of the last fifteen months of my life, this was a huge anti-climax. For weeks, I pondered the idea of going back to Bombay. But the question always was—*go back and do what?*

Despite that, I thought of my parents often. I knew my father felt terrible about putting me under such heavy pressure right out of college. He was calling me much more than he used to—and in those days, trunk calls were made across the oceans. On each call, he insisted, 'Shripal, don't worry. Don't take what I said to heart. Don't get stressed. If you want anything, we will support you.'

But for the first time, I was realizing the immense pressure of supporting my family, of realizing that they were dependent on me—and more heartbreakingly, that my aspirations could break them.

I may not have liked my job, but that didn't matter.

My family mattered.

In the meantime, while I was at Burt Reynolds, we had access to make free calls. Taking advantage of this, I called Bob Bishop one day and said that I wanted to meet him since I had potential investment schemes in mind with Burt Reynolds.

The generous gentleman he was, Bob gave me an appointment that very day.

He came straight to the point and asked me if I was enjoying the job.

'No,' I replied without preamble.

What happened next was, yet again, divine luck.

Of his own volition, Bob rang up the HR department at the NYSE and fixed an appointment for me for the next day. That night, I stayed at the YMCA. I didn't go in to work at Burt Reynolds the next day. Instead, I went for my interview. I was referred without delay to John Phelan, the president of the New York Stock Exchange.

Minutes into the interview, he hired me as his executive assistant, and I said 'yes' without thinking twice. Amused, he asked, 'don't you at least want to know your salary?'

'No,' I replied, 'I want to work here and I want to learn from you.'

Perhaps I *should* have asked him what my salary would be. When I got my appointment letter, my salary was only $1,500 per month. It was the same amount I had made doing odd jobs. But I braced myself. I would work extremely hard and work my way up.

The next day, I was back at my favourite NYSE. I did not dare to inform Burt Reynolds. I remained absent from work!

At my new job, I was given a small table, just next to the president's cabin. His chief advisor was a German lady. Apart from her, there were two secretaries. One of them was Debbie—short for Deborah Phelps. Twenty years my senior, she was an exceptionally beautiful woman. Moreover, she was kind and ensured I was comfortable.

This time around, my heart and soul were focused on the job. I might not have been earning much—but the NYSE was where I had always wanted to be. Within a month, the president was impressed by my work. Slowly, instead of going to the second-in-command, work began finding its way to my desk. Phelan wanted my inputs, enjoying my speed, clarity and the simplicity of the solutions I offered. He began handing me more responsibility. That's when I realized that this was how I was going to grow in life—by working under the most powerful person at the NYSE.

On the flip side, I was in for scathing barbs at the job. There were sixteen or seventeen vice presidents under Phelan, including Bob Bishop. The vice presidents felt that I was feeding the reports. All the reports would come to me, and I would send them with my comments. But I was just doing my job. My boss used to always tell me, 'the job you are in is the worst. People will hate you; they can bitch you out because they are your seniors but remember you are *my* EA.'

And for this nugget of privilege, I did not mind being taunted, did I?

As I progressed, my boss asked me to take a test. It was a test that specialists are required to take at NYSE, which acquaints one with all the responsibilities of a specialist market-maker. It was a difficult test and if you were proficient, at best you scored 60–65 per cent. Wary of exams, I studied hard over a weekend and got 98 per cent on that specialized test. More importantly, I completed the test in less than fifteen minutes, while my seniors struggled with the answers.

'You are back already?' My boss was surprised to see me back at my desk. Two hours later, he was elated at my score. It was an extraordinary moment. I was delighted beyond belief and also a little annoyed at myself. Why, I asked myself severely, was I stopping myself from moving ahead in life, simply because I was scared of the GMAT? By the looks of this test score, I was scared of very little in life! That weekend, I found myself studying for GMAT. My life was divided between the NYSE and my room.

By this time, I had shifted to Flushing in Queens. Here, room rentals were low, and crime rates were high. But for some reason, it was popular with Indians who were just about to start their lives in the US. The first thing you did in Queens was to change the lock since duplicate keys were always with someone else. At least, that's what everyone else told me. But being me, I ignored that piece of salient advice. One weekend, I returned from shopping for groceries to find my tiny apartment empty. That's how I learned—rather bitterly—that the first thing one does when one comes to live in Queens is to change the lock.

But even this couldn't defeat my sudden optimism. I continued to work and study, despite my recent losses. Three months later, I scored 96 per cent on the GMAT. The first thing I did after that was to apply for a doctoral programme at an Ivy League university. Guess what? I was accepted on probation. I would have to redo thirty-odd credits, but I didn't care. I was going to go to one of the best Ivy League universities in the world!

This was in November 1980. I chose to keep the news to myself for the time being and did not even share it with my parents or well-meaning colleagues. I wanted to focus on work where I was moving from strength to strength.

A career-defining moment came from a rather unfortunate incident. In March 1981, an assassination attempt was made on the then US President, Ronald Reagan. It happened at a time when the entire senior management at the NYSE had gone to Boca Raton for a conference. The markets began to plummet as news came in of a wounded President for whom age was not on his side. There were so many orders of sale on the stock exchange. Most of the stocks had reached their 'circuits', lowest permitted daily decline after which the stock is suspended for trading for the day. So I called my boss, and said, 'things are not looking good. We need to bring trade to a halt.'

Instantly, he replied, 'stop trading and just keep me posted every ten minutes.'

I immediately pressed the button to suspend trading. The tickers came to a standstill and faded to black. Now that trading was suspended by the NYSE, we had to send the information to the SEC. It was my first time drafting the letter. At Phelan's request, I went around the NYSE, assuring people that the markets would open soon. At that moment, I had all the power in the world, and it was intoxicating. The markets opened in less than two hours. But suspending trading had avoided a lot of financial damage, especially when President Reagan was declared to be out of danger by his medical staff and the market rebounded.

By now I had started consuming alcohol on rare occasions like office parties, so that I could blend in. That evening, I treated myself to a screwdriver, the classic combination of vodka and orange juice—as I wanted to celebrate a career-defining moment.

Soon after the incident, I was featured in the *New York Times*, lauded by my colleagues and seniors. It was a huge moment for me. Could this be the big high everyone talked about?

A few days later, I went to the Ivy League business school for a campus visit. I felt I was in the presence of Ma

Saraswati herself. I was as comfortable here as I was in the stock exchanges. My doctoral programme was centred around the importance of the development of global capital markets. I felt that I would be able to contribute and add value through the doctoral programme with my hands-on experience at two crucial financial capitals of the world: 1) Bombay—in a then underdeveloped economy, and 2) New York—in the world's most muscular economy.

I wanted to be rich desperately. The years I had spent struggling in America, as well as my parents' financial distress, had all served to teach me that money could smooth out the roughest path. An excellent way to get there was to have a pedigree from an Ivy League university and some influential contacts among the privileged. It sounds cold and calculating, and to a certain extent, I suppose it was. But I had had enough of struggling and barely making ends meet. I wanted to make my parents happy and proud, and I wanted to live a life of ease and comfort. I think we all want that at some level.

When he heard the news, my father's pride knew no bounds! His son was going to be an Ivy League student! I told him about the former Indian students who had studied there.

However, my admission was not on scholarship. I would have to pay fees and my parents lacked resources. That is when I turned to the trust fund that Smita and her friends had given me to manage. Seven of them had contributed $1,000 each and one individual pooled in $3,000. The only (rather large) problem was that this money was to be invested in shares and stocks. But it was the exact amount I had to pay to secure a seat at the Ivy League. I had, in my mind, no choice.

So I lied to Smita and her friends. I gave them bogus accounts, while using the money to pay university fees (I would show them that not only was I doing very well, but I was making 1.5 per cent –2 per cent returns for them). My whole idea was

that from the second semester onwards, I would tell them—
look, this is how I utilized your funds.

'*Baad main issey do gunha de doonga*', I told myself, '*lekin abhi mujhe yeh paiso ki zyada zaroorat hai*'. (I will double it and return it to them later. But right now, I need the money.)

So determined was I to get the Green Card that I started meeting girls of Indian origin . . . to take the easy way out of getting a permanent residency in USA.

* * *

But life had other plans. On 12 May 1981, I entered the office to find the receptionist waiting for me, looking confused. She told me that there had been umpteen calls from Bombay.

The matter, she said, seemed to be urgent.

I had a sinking feeling in the pit of my stomach. I had never received so many calls from home.

My cousin answered the call. He told me that my father was unwell.

'Has he passed away? Tell me the truth!' was my instinctive demand.

'No, no, he is not well, you just . . .'

Before he could continue, my sister came on the line. 'We have lost everything, Shripal!' she snapped and hung up. I remember clinging to the receiver, listening to the crackle of silence down the line.

This was it.

The moment it all ended.

5

Coming Back to India

. . . Your soul and mine are the same

We appear and disappear in each other.

—Rumi

May 1981–September 1985

It sank in when the flight was taxiing down the runway.

My dreams of settling in America, of building a life for myself here, were over. Tears came to my eyes as I looked out of the small oval window.

'You've made the right decision,' my boss remarked when I came to see him with the news. 'You must do what your heart tells you to. At this moment, don't use your brain.'

Logically speaking, he was right, of course, but logic didn't stop my tears.

A tall, burly young man crying copiously in that tiny plane seat must have been quite a sight. The air hostesses were staring at me. I cried non-stop through the sixteen-hour journey.

At half past midnight on 14 May 1981, I reached Bombay. It was a black moonless night. My cousin received me at the airport with a warm sympathetic hug. The way he looked into my red eyes, I knew . . . I was the head of the family now! My family consisted of my twenty-six-year-old, unmarried elder sister, a younger brother who was eighteen at the time, and my fifty-five-year-old mother. In those days, my sister had broken up with her fiancé, who happened to be my best friend in college. The separation was an acerbic one. On top of that, she'd now lost her father. My brother had just finished his grade XII board exams and was awaiting his results. He wanted to be a doctor. My parents had been together for forty years and I couldn't imagine how my mother felt being a widow at the relatively young age of fifty-five.

I had to be the rock they needed. I was only twenty-one. I wanted to be free, pursuing my dreams in America without a care in the world. But that was not meant to be.

Nor was there any time for personal grief. Other things broke me. For one, I realized that my father had already been cremated by my younger brother.

That was that.

I had not even been able to say goodbye—nor had I been able to fulfil my obligations as an elder son, to perform my father's last rites. He had done so much for me—and at the end, when I should have been there, I was away; not at his side.

It took me a short conversation with my mother, to realize that we were in a far worse situation than my father had let on. Firstly, nobody in the immediate family had any clue about income, household, or office expenses. After my father's death, people came to my mother, claiming to be creditors, demanding the return of money they said they had loaned my father. She had no idea about any of this, and understandably, she was shaken beyond words. The bank accounts had been in his name. There was no nominee, and no joint holder. The banks froze our accounts.

Worse, the capital obtained from selling Shakuntal had gone, vanished without a trace. When I investigated, I was told that it had been used to pay off the losses incurred by one of his sub-broker's clients.

To say that I was aghast is an understatement. I had promised my mother that I would sort things out, but how was I supposed to get all of us out of this mess? Where did I start?

* * *

After a sleepless first night back home, I woke early and went into office the next day. I couldn't help notice the difference. Just days ago, my office had been a tastefully done-up cabin with a seat next to the president of the New York Stock Exchange. Now I was shut in a bleak room, with paint cracking and peeling off the walls. The average age of staff in this organization was fifty-five. The mood was gloomy. An old, loyal accountant, working with us since my grandfather's days, came by for a cup of tea.

'Go back to the US,' he said, 'do something there. Business in Bombay is coming to a grinding halt. There is no future for you here.' The words struck fear in my heart, but I pushed it aside. I wasn't going to leave my family; I was determined about that. They needed someone to be their anchor. If that meant giving up on my dreams, then so be it.

Family would always come first for me now.

Nor was I going to take the accountant's advice and close down the business. I wanted to take a chance at reviving everything that had been lost. Soon I learned that the cousin to whom I had given the responsibility of running SSKY had left and had started his own venture in footwear and SSKY was shut. Had SSKY been up and running the way I had left it, it would have been a good source of income that could have taken care of my immediate financial needs.

I got down to business right away and started looking for sub-brokers. To take the quickest route to gather revenue, appointing sub-brokers who already had a pre-existing network of clients, was my best option.

I took a two-pronged strategy: the first was to reconnect and motivate the existing network of sub-brokers and the second was to build a fresh network of sub-brokers as well. It was, in essence, starting from scratch, but I was left with no other option. If there was one thing that my life had taught me, it was how to keep at something until I succeeded. I was no stranger to starting from scratch, after all.

Simply put, that is how within seven months, income gradually started trickling in.

But what about the capital? Well, my grandmother, in her wisdom, had divided the offices into three parts. She claimed that two parts belonged to my uncles, which was an incorrect decision, and my father who never went against her wishes had accepted it. It went against my father's interests, in my opinion. But then again, perhaps I speak out of turn. After all, I never really had the full picture.

Anyway, the new owners paid me a lakh to pass it on to my grandmother. However, I did not do what was necessary. I felt it belonged to the business. So I used it as seed capital to restart the company's engines. Again, doing so took me back to when I used the trust funds to pay my university fees in the United States. I remember that it had pricked my conscience back then, but it was in my opinion, something that had needed to be done. So I had done it. I applied the same logic to the present crises. After all, I had to make ends meet for my family . . . my mother, brother and sister.

It was a dangerous method. Perhaps I should have thought more carefully about it. As these things often do, if you don't watch out, it could become a way of life.

The second step I took was to recultivate my old underwriting contacts. It was yet another revenue stream that I could utilize. As business began to pick up slowly, the earnings were quite good.

Within three months, the number of sub-brokers had increased. I began to feel a little more comfortable. I was providing the same quality of life to my brother, sister and mother as my father had provided them. I could certainly never fill the vacuum he had left behind, but at least I was able to provide for them.

Like everything else in my life had been up until that moment, this feeling was short-lived.

If finances were stabilizing slowly, emotions were not. My family was grieving and they needed me constantly. But I had thrown myself into work as soon as I returned to India and I didn't have the mental and emotional bandwidth to handle my family 24x7. After all, I myself hadn't had the time to grieve the immense vacuum my father had left in my life. There were times when I would just come home and lock myself in my bedroom. I didn't want to see anyone. I didn't want to talk to anyone. In retrospect, I was immature and ill-equipped to handle the situation. But I simply didn't have the energy or bandwidth to deal with my family as all my energy was spent to revive my father's business.

As you can imagine, the stress and anxiety I was labouring under found its outlet—rage. My temper became uneven, often meteoric. I would snap at people; other times, I would break down in tears. Today, a therapist would diagnose me as suffering from acute depression. But in those days, I had no idea. All I knew was that I was constantly running on adrenaline and fumes. I had no energy to be compassionate, to be emotionally available, to be anything except tired.

To make matters worse—my younger brother scored only 75 per cent in his grade XII. These grades were not up to the mark for a medical college in Bombay. My cousin, an orthopaedic surgeon, suggested options like Belgaum and Manipal in Karnataka. I knew it would cost me a lot of money, but I didn't know how much.

My family began to panic. Where was I going to get the money from, they demanded. Their questions made my anxiety skyrocket. I knew that despite my best attempts, we had no reserves of cash just yet. The coffers were empty.

It was not like I was not doing my bit. I was trying with small as well as big gestures to the best of my ability to live up to everyone's expectations.

But I think over three months, my anger had reached disproportionate levels. It stemmed from grief and frustration at the unfairness of life. I had forfeited my dream at the altar of responsibility. Moreover, my education and my job experience in New York were not helping me here in India in any way. This business required leadership. In the state of mind I was in, I was not able to lead efficiently.

Frankly, I was not enjoying the business. It bruised my ego that from a position of power in the New York Stock Exchange, I wasn't even a speck of dust at the Bombay Stock Exchange. And every evening in the shower I would wonder when and how this speck of dust would become the universe of the Bombay Stock Exchange. My ambitions were always larger than life, but at that point, there didn't seem to be a way to fulfil them. I wanted to run away.

My fears led to an ugly fight at home. My brother, frustrated and young himself, shouted bitterly that he didn't want to be a doctor. That, more than anything, gave me the shock I needed.

It was almost as though my own heart had stopped beating. Had it come to this? Had my bitterness and anxiety driven us all to the point where my brother was on the verge of compromising his own dreams? Had I failed my family to the point where I couldn't even provide my brother with the education he wanted and needed?

There was no time to answer these questions.

We simply didn't have the money to send my brother to medical school.

So he decided to graduate from Jai Hind College. He told me he wanted to pursue his post-graduation from the United States like me. Oddly, it was almost as though *I* was the one getting a second chance—not my brother. His dreams felt suddenly like my own. That day, as we talked things through, I promised him—by hook or by crook—I would send him to the United States.

Around this time, my mother was approached by an acquaintance of the Lalbhai family. The Lalbhais were wealthy textile tycoons and philanthropists based in Ahmedabad. They were looking for a suitable groom for their daughter Kalpana. On paper, it made sense to approach our family. Our respective grandfathers had not only known each other, but each man had had mutual respect for the legacy the other had created. The great Kasturbhai Lalbhai had inaugurated my grandfather's Shakuntala Kantilal Ishwarlal Jain Girls' High School. Both families were Jains and both had known one another for over three generations.

Not surprisingly, they asked about me. When my mother told me of their conversation, I wondered why the Lalbhai family would want a pauper like me for a son-in-law.

I found out later, that they were under the impression that though our fortunes had dwindled, we had substantial wealth in investments in gold. From those they cared to ask, they heard the Gujarati phrase '*Bhanjyu toea Bharuch*', which meant, 'even if the wealthy city of Bharuch faced losses, there would always be something substantial left over'. The truth, of course, was that we were not rich by any means. I'm pretty sure if the Lalbhais had known the reality of what lay behind our reputation, that marriage would never have been solemnized.

When I was introduced to Kalpana, I was drawn to her simplicity, despite her family's towering financial and business status. She was so straightforward and honest that I wanted to spend all my time with her from the moment we met. The twenty-two-year-old in me wanted to escape his loneliness. A companion as direct and compassionate as Kalpana, I felt, would bring back the sparkle missing in my life.

But for all that I appreciated *her* honesty, I was not honest with her. I didn't dare tell her the truth about the true state of either my mental health or our finances. Thankfully for me, she was a smart young woman. Within a month, she had gauged independently that we were not as well off as our reputation suggested. Nor, she realized, did my sister like her very much. We didn't know then that my sister was falling prey to the monster that is schizophrenia. For now, we merely thought that it was a sibling's jealousy of her dearest brother being shared—coupled with the bitterness over her own break-up.

On the other hand, my brother took an instant liking to Kalpana and the two started to build a bond of their own. He looked up to her and she showered him with love and respect.

While I was happily basking in the companionship of my fiancée, my lack of finances was making me more insecure than ever. Kalpana knew that we were not in the best financial condition, and it put further pressure on me. I had to be successful for my wife at all costs. She must, I was determined, keep enjoying the same comforts and lifestyle she had known at her parents' home. *'Unke jaisa banna hi padega'* (I must be as good as them, if not better) became my sole aim.

I started borrowing heavily from family members. At first, I renovated my bedroom. I did not have an air-conditioner, so I got one installed. Next, I planned a honeymoon in Mauritius. She had not asked for a foreign destination and was perfectly content with an Indian hill station, but I wanted to show off. Then I purchased a second car for the two of us. All of this was on borrowed money and it made me feel poorer by the day, and more anxious than ever before. If you had asked me how I intended to pay any of this back, I couldn't have given you a straight answer as I didn't know. All I knew was that I wanted to show the world that I could and would give Kalpana a comfortable lifestyle—the same as the one she had always known.

I was in a headlong rush to prove I was rich enough for Kalpana. And there was no one to stop me. Looking back, it was my ego that landed me knee-deep in debt.

Three months after our engagement, I felt an acute pain in my chest. I was rushed to the hospital, where tests revealed that my heartbeat was arrhythmic. The cardiologist bluntly told me it was a severe threat to my life and I could die with no warning. It was so simply put that it took my breath away.

For a moment, I sat there, paralysed.

I was twenty-two and about to get married—and I could die at any point. My cousin took me elsewhere for a second opinion and then for a third. The diagnosis remained unchanged.

I was going out of my mind. The idea of death and dying plagued my waking hours.

But even here, I couldn't tell Kalpana.

What if she left me? Who would want to marry a dying man?

On the sly, I kept visiting different doctors, praying that at least one would tell me differently.

But their advice didn't change: 'Your lifespan is unpredictable. We advise cancelling or at least postponing the wedding.'

Inevitably, Kalpana noticed a change in my behaviour. I was withdrawn, moody, depressed.

Gently, one day, she asked me what the matter was.

The gentleness broke me down.

In tears, I finally told her the truth.

If I had expected her to leave, I was mistaken. She was calm—but very firm. I had to go to her city, Ahmedabad, and visit her cousin who was a heart specialist. I didn't know what he would tell me that a legion of doctors in Mumbai hadn't already told me, but I went anyway.

Her home was grand. Her bathroom was bigger than my bedroom. Outside the room I was allotted, there was a garden with peacocks sauntering about. It was a stark contrast from the crows cackling outside my balcony in Mumbai. Overwhelmed, I felt tears rising to my throat. I was a spiritually and emotionally broken man, with a constant fear of death. What sort of hell was I dragging her into? It was around that time that I finally had a heart-to-heart—excuse the pun—with Kalpana. I asked her honestly if she still wanted to marry me. We had time to call off the wedding. She could have a chance at a better life, with a better, more healed man. Kalpana heard me out patiently, then she asked me never to ask her that question ever again. She was kind and loving right through it all. Her unconditional acceptance of me along with my many flaws was beyond logic.

With my mind more at rest, at least as far as her love for me was concerned, I began to look around me more objectively. The Lalbhais were very different from us, in how they ate, spoke and behaved. For example, for the first four trips to Ahmedabad, I barely got 10 per cent of what I needed to satisfy my appetite. Finally one day, the legendary Kasturbhai Lalbhai's sister noticed my voracious appetite. Since then, whenever I was around, the rules of how much had to be cooked and how to serve were changed. I also realized that the Lalbhais might be a financially prominent family, but they were heaven-sent and a rarity in this world.

Kalpana's cousin in Ahmedabad gave me a clean bill of health. I felt I had been resurrected back to life. It would be years before Kalpana told me the real truth. Her cousin had actually warned her not to marry me. 'Do not marry him; I do not know how long he is going to live. His uneven beat could lead to death at any given point in time,' the cousin had said. I still do not know why Kalpana chose to be with me, despite knowing the truth.

Kalpana and I were married in December 1981. It had only been six months since my father had passed away. Life was moving at breakneck speed. So much had happened since then. I had lost everything: a parent, a dream, money . . .

And yet in Kalpana, I saw the promise of a new beginning. Her presence motivated me to do better than my best. As arranged, we went to Mauritius on our honeymoon to usher in our married life. The first night, we lived life king-size in a posh five-star hotel, facing the ocean. The next night we had to move to a smaller hotel in the heart of town, far away from the beach. I had only had money for one night's stay in a luxury hotel. Kalpana did not make a fuss; in fact, she said nothing.

We came back to Bombay and started settling into the marriage. My cousin's sister was going to be married next, so everyone in the family was busy with that.

Life seemed to be settling into a rhythm.

How mistaken I was!

Back in the early 1980s, Sumatilal Jamnadas was one of the biggest brokers of the Bombay Stock Exchange. Do you remember my favourite uncle, Biju mama, the author? S.J., as he was known as, was Biju mama's wife's brother. S.J. ran a speculative bubble in Century Textile's shares. Although he was an extremely intelligent man, his ego had taken over and irrespective of the situation he did not change his stance. It was around this time that I discovered that my firm's clients were short on Century. We were contractually obligated to receive some Rs 8 lakh from them. But before that sum could come in, S.J. declared bankruptcy. It was my firm's responsibility to pay the clients. I was in tears. If I lost Rs 8 lakh to him, my firm would go bankrupt.

However, Sumatilal Jamnadas could not help. I told my mother about my losses. We would need to sell her jewellery to bridge the deficit. It was the last of our remaining wealth. We called my cousin's sister who was now a newlywed bride. Her husband was a jeweller. We sold a chunk of family heirloom jewellery for a price of Rs 4 lakh. My in-laws helped me to the extent of Rs 1.5 lakh. That increased the amount to Rs 5.5 lakh and I scraped together the remainder from customer advances and capital.

I was barely recovering from the loss when, three months later, a bigger nightmare came my way. The broker, Harkishandas Laxmidas, had accumulated a large portion of Tata Iron and Steel Corporation Limited (TISCO) and its shares were falling like an avalanche. None of us expected this firm to go down so swiftly. After all, it had its investment banking division, brokerage division and high net worth clients. It was amongst the top four holistic broking firms, one that I wanted to emulate.

The silver lining was that our exposure was only Rs 1.5 lakh. Yet again, we sold more gold to pay off the balance. At that time, I realized that I had to do other things to create a substantial income for myself and my family.

The back-to-back failures made me very bitter and anxious. I would, albeit unfairly, unload my frustrations at work on my wife. I was obnoxious and picked fights with her and her family members.

During that period, it seemed as though whatever I touched was turning to dust. I ignored my traditional businesses. I began a new underwriting channel, because of shortage of funds. My income from brokerage had gone down substantially in this uncertain phase. To top it all off, Kalpana told me that soon we would be parents. She was now visibly concerned. How were we to bring a child into this world when I was struggling to this degree?

Every Wednesday, my father-in-law made a trip to Bombay for his weekly meetings. When Kalpana confided in him about her pregnancy, he beamed with pride and joy. But she put paid to that joy quickly. She wanted to abort the child, she confessed. There was no way she could be a mother when her world and her life with me was fraught with so much tension. Her father explained gently that every child comes into this world with his own karma. He asked his daughter to have faith in god. God would never let her down, he promised.

Uncertain but wanting to do her best, Kalpana kept the child. She must have wished valiantly that she had made different choices in her life. As my mental health spiralled, I knew I was losing control of my mind and emotions. There were times when even Kalpana, normally so patient and loving, could not bear to be with me. I knew that I had to be caring because Kalpana's mental and emotional health was doubly important now. But despite this, I couldn't control my temper. With my financial position shaky again, I was on the brink of a complete collapse.

Kalpana gave birth to a baby girl. When I held my daughter in my arms for the first time, I just broke down. The mental agony that I had put my wife through had not affected my child. One glance at her opened my eyes. I knew I wanted to always be around for my daughter and my wife. I embraced Kalpana. But this time, my wife did not move. She then told me that during her pregnancy, she had told her family the truth of all the anguish I was causing her at home. Her family was aghast and they promised her that they would support her if she chose to leave me.

That's exactly what she chose.

My wife moved to Ahmedabad with my daughter. She was going to call it quits. We did not contact each other for over a month. I couldn't think of anything beyond them while she was gone. Finally, I gave up even trying. I booked a flight to Ahmedabad. Once I landed, I stayed in a hotel. I didn't know whether she would even see me, but Kalpana wasn't that sort of woman.

She brought our baby girl into our room and my heart melted. She was a tiny gurgling bundle of joy and I cried copiously as I lifted her into my arms. Kalpana sat quietly and watched us.

Later, she would tell me that it was the emotion I showed that day that made her decide to come back to Bombay.

A few days later, my daughter was burning with fever. The paediatrician, Kalpana's relative, came for a home visit. As she wrote the prescription, she looked at the air-conditioner and said, 'Kalpana, you are such an idiot. Switch on the AC and keep it at 21 degrees Celsius.' Kalpana nodded but said nothing as she knew that the air-conditioner didn't even work. My financial position was so dismal that I did not have money to repair it.

During that time, Richard Attenborough's celluloid masterpiece *Gandhi* was released and I took my entire family to see the film.

Maybe it was Gandhiji's philosophy, and the problems he went through that drew me into his spell. I was so influenced by the film that, for the first time, I put aside my ego, and prepared to work with my wife's brother.

I told my wife, 'Kalpana, I am not just at rock bottom, I am scraping it. I can either be a scavenger or a thief. I need to meet with your family, learn something, and then make my mark in the world.'

Kalpana first spoke with her mother. My mother-in-law was a very strong lady and took the news with as much equanimity as could be expected. But Kalpana's father, who loved his daughter, was shattered to hear she was in such a dire situation. I didn't blame him. I would feel the same, if I had been her father. Between us, we spoke to my brother-in-law, who had just started managing the business empire. He agreed to help out to the extent of Rs 10,000 every month. Kalpana asked her brother if he could find a job for me.

In the meantime, my daughter was growing into a lovely toddler. I would take her to Hanging Gardens every morning. As the days passed, I began to feel better about myself. My financial pressure was assuaged because of the Rs 10,000 coming in at the end of every month. I told my brokerage firm, 'Look here, you manage everything. If there is any deficiency, I will close the business. I can no longer fund deficits.'

It was around this time when Hotel President, one of the first five-star hotels in south Mumbai, opened its doors. One of its best restaurants was Trattoria, known for its authentic Italian cuisine. When my daughter was around nine months old, we decided to go there for dinner. The bill, I remember with stark clarity, was Rs 956. I was only thinking in terms of numbers in those days—and '956' was almost 10 per cent of what came in at the end of every month. Both I and my wife were so guilty about that single dinner, that we didn't visit any fine dining restaurants for a long, long time!

Finally, as a good Samaritan, my brother-in-law came to my rescue and introduced me to a gentleman called Ravi Ratan Arora. He was from IIM Ahmedabad and not only was he a very intelligent man, but he also taught me a lot. My brother-in-law was starting a leasing company and I became one of its first employees. It was called Anagram Finance Limited. My learning graph was steep, but I wanted to become wealthy. I had a daughter to raise and a brother whom I wanted to send to the United States for his education. I started working extremely hard. My financial support was solely the Rs 10,000 my wife gave me every month. I rarely went to my stock exchange office now. I used to call up in the evening to find out what the brokerage was and keep a strong vigil on client receivables. Otherwise, I was completely wedded to this new job at Anagram.

At that time, I did not know how to evaluate the company as even audited reports did not represent the true financial position of the company. What were the systems that would be needed to set up for this? We went to friendly companies and sold them an audacious scheme. Two companies purchased the schemes and this resulted in soaring profits for Anagram Finance.

However, I felt a bit suffocated.

But what bothered me even more was that I did not know my end game. How was this going to end for me? How was this going to benefit me?

And yet I was learning a lot especially from the way my brother-in-law was handling his business challenges.

I must admit this was a relatively stable period of my life. I went with my in-laws, my wife and daughter, for a small holiday in Matheran. I spoke a lot with my mother-in-law and we became close. She had several health issues, but in my conversations with her, I realized that, as I've mentioned before, she was one of the strongest and most practical women that I knew. To imbibe 'true education' into her son and daughter, she started a school with many extracurricular activities. There was a glow about her and a magic in her voice which was inexplicable. I wanted to be a child again and put my head in her lap, so that all my worries would just melt away.

My father-in-law was a true Gandhian and someone who implemented Jain philosophy as a way of life. He was the most approachable human being I had met and my antidote to depression. Just fifteen minutes in his presence would envelope me in a sense of well-being. He became my guru in the absence of my father. His advice was simple and spiritual. It was my loss that I did not implement his teachings in my life.

A person looks good and feels good when he is truly loved. Back then, I had lost weight and was looking younger than my years. I had lost 42 kilos and my waist had whittled down to 30 inches. I made a conscious decision to take care of myself as I had a daughter and a wife.

People would tell my wife, 'you married a man and he has become a boy!'

Soon we celebrated my daughter's first birthday and the entire family came together. My sister was close to my daughter, though she continued to blow hot and cold with my wife. On the other hand, my wife and brother got along well. She assured him that he was like her son and would not have another child. I was not around when she told him this. She was aware that he wanted to pursue his studies in America and supported him wholeheartedly.

If Kalpana wanted, she could have turned around and said that the money was coming in from her family. Why should she spend it on anyone other than the three of us? Yet, she continued to be wholly generous throughout, standing by me like a rock. I was determined to show her I was grateful.

At that time, I figured out a novel and ingenious way of making rich people's black money white using the Shell law that cost them peanuts in an era of high taxes. The idea was to start a public limited company in order to convert black money to white. I started four such companies, which earned me revenue of Rs 14 lakh and with that I got a small office in Maker Chambers 3. I started operating from there and for the first time, I hired staff.

I hired a company secretary, a compliance officer, a telephone operator, and a secretary. At that time, a new bank called the Bank of Credit and Commerce International (BCCI) had recently opened in town. The bank naturally wanted clients. I ensured to 'accidentally bump' into the credit manager one day, just for the opportunity to tell him that I could make a large reputed group in Western India their client. He was delighted and said it would be a privilege to meet the young scion of the group and figure they could collaborate.

So I fixed the appointment. This led to the bank granting this group, with an impeccable reputation, its banking facilities in four of its listed companies and many of their fledgling units. My cash registers started ringing as a result of the huge commissions. This was the start of a new business.

Then, I came across a well-known bank from the Middle East with whom I built a great rapport. I realized then that you could spin cock-and-bull stories just for the sake of building bonds! I fine-tuned the art, and soon, I was getting bank limits to increase liquidity for my existing clients. Over time, I brought on board twenty new clients. Soon, the business was booming beyond my wildest imagination. For the first time in my life, I was making Rs 3–4 lakh a month. Every evening, I perused my balance sheet and made a note of my surplus fund. Now that I had money at my disposal, I renovated my stock exchange office and the Nariman Point office.

I told my brother to start preparing for the application process for universities in the United States. He was completely clueless about how to begin or even what he wanted to do. He decided eventually to follow in the footsteps of Kalpana's cousin, who was studying engineering in Boston.

With my brother's career set and enough money in the bank, I finally felt as though I was the head of the family. Now, my *fufaji*—my father's sister's husband—came to *me* for help. It was a big turnaround. He told me that his son-in-law was going through a tough time in his small-scale chemical business. Could I help?

I was happy to. By the grace of god, the one thing I am proud of even today is that I have not refused to help anyone in distress. I told my fufaji that I would make his son the head of my firm, SSKI. He would be the business development officer as I did not have the time to attend to the broking business.

For the first time in my life, the broking business started looking up under a new dedicated leadership. My cousin didn't know anything about the business, initially. But he was a fast learner, and soon, the number of clients began to increase.

The tide had turned in my favour.

Finally.

6

Flying High

You were born with wings

Why prefer to crawl through life.

—Rumi

1990–1999

During the mid to the late 1980s, companies were created on the Bombay Stock Exchange to convert black money into white. A company would be formed and floated for a public issue. The capital base on offer would range from Rs 5 lakh to Rs 25 lakh. The investment banker would collect cash (black money) from one party who needed white money. He would find various 'subscribers' who had 'cash in hand' to subscribe to the shares of this company. They would deposit cash and apply for a subscription. If I recollect correctly, in those days, a public limited company required twenty subscribers for every five lakh of issuance. The issue would be subscribed to when it opened for listing. It was listed at face value and over some time, the price quoted was down from Rs 10 to a few annas. At this time, the shares would be picked up by the person wishing to convert his black money to white. He obtained control of a company at a few annas per share, his total cost coming to approximately less than 10 per cent. He was thus able to convert his black money to white at one-fourth of the then prevailing income tax rate.

I got contracts from four such people who had excessive cash and wanted my services to convert them into shares. I earned around Rs 14 lakh from that operation. During that time, there was a huge financial crunch in the country amongst small to medium-sized corporates. Even emerging corporates like Reliance Industries were going through a cash crunch, because of the archaic procedure that banks used to decide on the working capital.

Many companies resorted to selling their goods to an affiliate against which their consortium bankers would give them funds. The affiliate would then sell the goods to a third party and a bill of exchange would be discounted by a foreign bank. Similarly, raw material purchases were financed through bills of exchange. Thus, they got two-and-a-half to three times the financing for the same goods. Many companies in my portfolio even floated 'bogus bills' of exchange where no goods were involved. In this way, some ingenious Marwari entrepreneurs were able to avail of financing that never appeared in their books.

I happened to make inroads into two foreign banks, one of which is defunct today. My days were usually spent at the bank trying to explain the creditworthiness of companies that were in fact not creditworthy.

It was an easy way to make money without putting in capital and my clients increased over time. I had a bagful of clients, ranging from textile companies to EPC (engineering, procurement and construction) companies to metal companies. In every sector, some of the most rotten apples from that industry became a part of my portfolio. Thus, their survival was solely in my hands. In the process, I not only made money but also felt powerful. My interest arbitrage was on the upswing and my net interest income was higher than some of the best banks operating in those days. The business skyrocketed to Rs 25 crore per month.

Finally, in 1983–84, I could afford to send my brother to the United States for further studies. He studied engineering in Boston and got an MBA from New York. He was in the US for four years and I was able to fund him effortlessly. I would also visit my brother two to three times a year, many times flying the Concorde from London to New York.

Now not only could I travel first class, but I was able to take my family for several international vacations. My father-in-law began joking that my daughter had seen more countries in her young life than he had seen in his lifetime.

I also started a leasing firm where many companies in need of replacement finance or finance to augment working capital by sale and lease back of assets would approach us. I crafted a niche of my own and would lend three to five years of resources at an exorbitant rate. Since their bill discounting was routed through me, recovery was never an issue. Our asset books grew to Rs 30 crore. We were on a steady rise. I increased my network of banks to include public sector banks.

In the meantime, our leasing operations expanded further. We moved to a new, larger, 2,000 square feet office at Free Press House. It was one of the most tastefully done-up offices I had seen in India, with a sea view.

We now shifted out of my family's four BHK apartment to an 800 square foot two BHK on Altamount Road. The move was primarily to give my mother more space to deal with my sister's increasing schizophrenia. It was still something we were trying to cope with. In those days, we did not know what schizophrenia was all about and I used to think it was a temper tantrum—jealousy triggered by my marriage, compounded by the grief of losing our father as well as her boyfriend, simultaneously. But as her mental health spiralled out of control, my mother advised Kalpana and me to move out, for the sake of our daughter.

Though the Altamount Road house was smaller than the family flat, the three of us lived in bliss. I think I would be right in calling it a love nest, no matter how fanciful that sounds. We hardly entertained outsiders as we did not have friends and kept to ourselves. I consider the Altamount Road house very auspicious.

It was also a period when everything in my life seemed to be flowing smoothly and I couldn't have been happier. The leasing operation was going well, my network of corporate contacts was growing, and relations with banks were on an upswing. In a nutshell, business was growing exponentially. Even the stock exchange business was garnering good revenues as my brother-in-law was able to add new clients and sub-brokers! However, despite the prosperity, it might sound strange to you, the reader, sleep still eluded me at night. Because the truth was—I was running a fake business.

I don't write those words lightly. All the bills that were discounted were fake. The letters of credit under which the bills were discounted were fake. No transactions had materialized. The bills of exchange were accommodation bills. This was legitimate at that time. However, it meant that the corporate debtor raised money twice for the same transaction. This anomaly was also pointed out later in the joint Parliamentary committee (JPC) headed by Ram Niwas Mirdha.

The promoters of these companies used to put undue pressure on me to raise more resources. Initially, I enjoyed the process but over a period it got tedious. To pay Peter, they had to rob Paul. I was their accomplice. On one occasion, a bank manager from a state-run bank also got suspended because of one of the accommodation bills discounted by the bank. Essentially, I was sleepless because I was guilty.

It should have been a sign. The bad times were just about to roll in . . .

After his graduation in the USA, my brother decided to return to Bombay and work with me. I welcomed him with open arms. From the beginning, he was my equal partner. But soon, things started to go wrong between the two of us.

At the time, the primary reason was that I wanted him to learn. Since we were so close, I thought he could read my mind. My associates had to be quick-witted and swift decision-makers like me. Didn't he understand my pressure to make as much money as possible? To keep clients happy? I knew the pulse of the business better than he did. I knew that, but the mistake I made was to keep losing my temper with him. I had a bad temper—and I lost it with my brother often. Little did I know that every time I was angry with him the chasm between us widened. Looking back, I realize that when he did the bill discounting along with me, he was either disinterested or perhaps he realized that it was a fake business that I was running. I still don't know what the reason for his half-heartedness was, but I always wished him well. When he decided to get married, I told him to move to a separate flat with his wife. I even bought him a three BHK flat in the same block of apartments where I lived. I was on the sixth floor and he was on the twelfth. I thought living in close proximity might help bring us closer.

I was wrong about that, as you will see—but I just wanted the best for my brother—and even today, he continues to be in my prayers.

Over time, greed got the better of me. In those days, Harshad Mehta* acquired liquidity from banks by issuing government security receipts where no security existed. A Marwari industrial client of mine was very close to a large investment banker who owned a small bank. This bank would issue fake receipts and were discounted by various banks. The scam stretched across the largest Indian bank, the largest US owned bank and a whole host of nationalized and small Indian banks. People were using this money to bet on stocks and the money was indeed cheap. In those days, an 8.99 per cent interest rate was a steal. This is how Harshad Mehta could take delivery of all his shares and create artificial scarcity so that the price of those shares would reach far beyond their true intrinsic value. Since I was already in the system, I had an idea.

With the blessings of my Marwari client and by utilizing our strong network in the financial sector, we developed a Rs 300 crore portfolio of *badla*, which gave us a profit of Rs 30 to 40 lakh a month.† So financially, it was the best period of my life. There was a sharp material improvement in my life, but subsequently, I lost sleep and peace of mind. My behaviour

---

* Harshad Mehta was an Indian stockbroker who orchestrated the 1992 security scam by manipulating the stock market by using fraudulent bank receipts representing ownership of government securities.

† *Badla* was an indigenous carry-forward system invented on the Bombay Stock Exchange as a solution to the perpetual lack of liquidity in the secondary market. Badla trading involved buying stocks with borrowed money with the stock exchange acting as an intermediary at an interest rate determined by the demand for the underlying stock and a maturity not greater than seventy days. Like a traditional futures contract, badla is a form of leverage. It was banned by the Securities and Exchange Board of India (SEBI) in 1993, effective March 1994.

was erratic. Why wouldn't it be? The entire foundation of my business was based on an unsustainable financial model. I was haunted by a premonition of impending doom . . . Six months after that premonition, the Harshad Mehta scam was unearthed with the help of a whistle-blower at India's largest nationalized bank, and Sucheta Dalal, a feisty journalist.

The media was in a tizzy. Harshad and his brother were arrested. Many officials of the US-based bank either quit or were fired. Mutual fund officials were under arrest . . . they were the same ones with whom my stock broking firm had started a business. The chairman of the largest public sector mutual fund and the CMO of a south-based bank passed away. Had they been alive, the scam and its repercussions would have been much worse.

I was on shaky ground because the only sustainable business I had was leasing. And that was under control because of bill discounting. What would happen to this portfolio once the bill discounting stopped? The receivables stopped coming in as the bill discounting business came to a grinding halt.

My fear levels were off the charts.

Fortunately, I had reduced the business to 10 per cent of its original size. Still, the losses incurred resulted in my entire capital being wiped out. The stock broking business was on pause as clients who followed Harshad Mehta had lost a fortune. My survival was at stake, but my survival instincts were at their peak. I ensured most of the stock broking clients paid in cash or kind. I ensured that the residual money receivables were realized by oscillating between persuasion and soft aggression. All companies, except for two, paid their receivables, so my exposure was down to less than a crore of rupees. I cleared all my bank liabilities by stopping the badla, which was done with the leader of the bear cartel. He was true to his word and released all the money in two months. This activity was the biggest source of my income, and it came to a grinding halt.

This way, before the scam reached its peak, I paid off the bulk of my liabilities. I had very limited capital and decided to lie low, but it was of no use.

One day, I made it to the front page of a newspaper, launched by India's largest industrial conglomerate today! Thrust into infamy, most criminal lawyers I met suggested that the chances of my arrest were high as the Central Bureau of Investigation was on an overdrive. Their retainer was steep as Harshad Mehta, financial institutions, the Reserve Bank of India, officials of financial institutions as well as individual brokers were all clamouring for their services. I decided against hiring them. I was willing to face the music, rather than pay a fortune for expensive lawyers.

Then in the 1992 JPC report on the Harshad Mehta scam, my leasing companies were blacklisted. The CEO of the Middle Eastern bank lost his job and though I was in no way responsible till date I feel the guilt of it.

The clock was ticking, slowly but persistently. My dark phase eclipsed the good times. In addition to the closure of our bill discounting business as well as our leasing business, we lost 50,000 shares of Reliance worth Rs 50 lakh then, which in today's market would be worth more than Rs 500 crore. Most importantly, we knew who had stolen the money, but we could not do anything about it. This was the first time our paperwork was weak.

It was during this time that the government was attaching properties of those accused in the Harshad Mehta scam. One of my Bandra (west) properties was seized by the income tax department as it was acquired from my Marwari client referred earlier. It took me six years to get it released from the IT department.

I was also worried about my brother. His flat was in the name of one of the companies that was mentioned in the JPC report. I was bending over backwards to get that property out of the mess as I cared deeply about him, but despite my best efforts, my brother was naturally panicking.

For two to three years, I was fighting one legal case after another. My income tax files were scrutinized. I was in London when the CBI raided my house. My wife was alone while they searched the place. I still do not know the reason for the raid. After I came back, I spoke to them on the phone. However, I was never summoned to their office.

In the meantime, India's coalition government, headed by Prime Minister P.V. Narasimha Rao introduced a scheme for foreign institutional investors to invest in India. It was my brother's brainchild, wherein he got us an association with Smith New Court, a Hong Kong-based firm that was later acquired by Merrill Lynch.

I did not interfere in that business at all. I was sapped of my energy, extremely anxious because my limited resources were fast depleting. It was a daunting time, emotionally as well as financially.

I was as fallible as anybody else. My wife and daughter faced the full brunt of my frustrations. My daughter was only four years old at this time and I'm ashamed to say that she was witness to my dark side. I was losing my temper on a whim. My depression and anxiety were at their peak. However, I did not know that it was depression back then—just as I could not understand my sister's schizophrenia. There was no concept of mental health awareness back then. I did not have the motivation to do business.

But somehow, I had the fortitude to face the crisis up front. I had the adequate paper trail to be given a clean chit by the authorities. Honestly speaking, I had not taken anyone's money. The entire principal along with interest had been paid back. I fought tooth and nail with many clients for premature repayments—even if it meant a small loss of the principal amount. Thus, within one month of the scam breaking out, I had successfully repaid a Rs 300-crore liability.

And though the CEO of the Middle Eastern bank had changed, I continued doing business with them.

But I was getting tired of this business. I was saddled with a reasonably large organization and no in-flow to speak of. I vowed to myself that my next endeavour would be an honest one.

The sleepless nights were not worth the money. The money that came in easily made its way out even faster. The idiom 'easy come easy go' kept ringing in my mind.

My brother and a consultant were running SSKI. They had tied up with a small foreign brokerage firm, headquartered in London, to attract foreign institutions. Their area of expertise was supposed to be researching reports and then procure institutional clients to whom they could sell stocks, covered by the reports. My brother did not hire research professionals or market experts. He just relied on the consultant and as a result the first research report was shoddy.

Smith New Court wrote a letter that the research was not only rudimentary but unprofessional as well. If the company was so disinterested, they were happy to discontinue. My brother came to me seeking help. I told him, 'This is not the way business is done. You must create a system and structure in the organization.' I got involved only to salvage the situation.

I appointed a CEO for the business along with five research analysts and I ensured I invested in great minds. As days rolled into months, we were among the first professionally-run research organizations! The CEO was a competent professional, but unfortunately I had to fire him, because my brother and he could not see eye to eye. I regretted my decision, but blood is thicker than water. Soon, I was running the SSKI-Smith New Court business. My brother was relegated to the sidelines and was extremely bitter. But I had no other option as the collaborators wanted me in. That only widened the existing rift between us as he felt I had taken over his business. But that was not my intention; I only wanted to revive and grow the business for him.

My brother was a bright guy. He started his career in investment banking with us. I will not take away that credit from him. He tapped small and mid-cap companies and asked if they needed capital and then pitched that SSKI had connections with foreign investors. At that time, foreign institutions were not interested in the stories of Reliance, Tata or Century; they were interested in small-cap stock and mid-cap stock because that is how markets across the globe grow.

With this operation, we used to enjoy a hefty 4 per cent on the placements. Every month, we would do placements worth Rs 20–25 crore. The tide had turned and the good phase had started once again. This was 1993–94 and we had become the largest institutional brokers with a 90 per cent market share. We had two strong clients: one from Scotland and the other from Hong Kong. Most of their purchases were through us because of our robust equation with our collaborators. Moreover, I made sure to build a personal rapport with them and soon, SSKI became a name to reckon with.

However, like any other business that I started, my dreams were larger than the financial resources at hand. That was the factor that brought me down on various occasions. If I had X resources, my commitments were X raised to the power of four. If that commitment was for a Friday, I would start working on it from Wednesday. I was not being lazy. I just did not want to be stressed so early on. My heartbeat would shoot up and the left side of my shoulder would hurt because of stress. I used to borrow money at 5 per cent monthly interest rates from players such as a defunct TV manufacturing company and a now defunct financial services company.

Then, Ketan Parekh*, held by many to be the second big scamster of modern India, started gathering momentum. Since 'K-10' stocks (recommended by him) was the gold rush of that time, both Indian and foreign investors lapped them up in the hope of making a fortune.

The now infamous promoter of a waste management and engineering, procurement and construction company, Nandan Gadgil, known for his flamboyance, was touted as the next big thing in the world of Indian business back in the mid-1990s. He had an engineering company and an operation that could make energy from waste material. He had shifted his base to Dubai.

One of his relatives was a client. We started working for him aggressively. We had institutional business and the business of the largest operator in the market. Unfortunately, I was low on resources and avoided paying the margin to the BSE. Now, whenever one does a position on behalf of a retail client, the brokerage firm is supposed to pay margins. Back then, I was so thin on resources and so desperate for revenue that I was unable to pay the margins which aggregated to Rs 2.5 crore at that time.

In those days, the settlement period was fifteen days and the clients had the option to take delivery or do 'badla'—which is forwarding their position for a fee to the short seller or someone who had the money to take delivery for a fortnight in consideration of a fee, on his behalf.

---

* Ketan Parekh was an Indian stockbroker who manipulated the prices of small-cap stocks using borrowed money, circular and insider trading.

For all carry-forward positions, there was a daily/bi-weekly margin and I made a conscious decision not to pay the margins. I thought to myself that even if I was caught, I could seek pardon.

Unfortunately, I was caught. The Marwari majority board wanted me to fail and fall. In the absence of SEBI, I had to pay a fine of Rs 79 lakh, though the previous highest fine was only Rs 3 lakh. Moreover, I was suspended for seven days which meant my registration with foreign institutional investors was cancelled. The lenders from whom I had borrowed for settlement were knocking on my door. Scant on liquidity, I was pushed against a wall.

I decided to use a three-pronged strategy. First, we approached various foreign firms for investment. India was not that hot as an investment destination then and the recent past came in the way of collaborations. Second, I met every domestic and foreign institutional investor to tell them 'Tiger zinda hain' (the tiger is alive), without knowing how I would survive. Lastly, I began a resource mobilization drive.

I had a liability of approximately Rs 36 crore. My team was crestfallen. I pleaded with them to give me a fortnight to resolve the issue. Just a year ago, I had lost my entire dealing room team to an international brokering home. Now, I did not want to lose my remaining team which I had built painstakingly. I had the best brains working in research and investment banking, and to lose them was to lose the value of my company.

Against all odds, I was able to raise Rs 15 crore from a private equity fund out of Singapore. This was when broking houses were not the flavour of the day. The finance company of India's largest industrial group gave me Rs 6 crore, but I still short of Rs 15 crore. I had no option but to approach my family. I had ample assets and agreed to transfer all my assets to them. That was their first precondition. The second pre-condition was that

I would be 'monitored' on a day-to-day basis. But I told them point blank, 'either you trust me, or don't give me the money'. It was too much of a humiliation being asked unnecessary questions by their second-in-command officials, just to see if I was doing anything illegal. I told him that they were more than adequately covered with two apartments, 50 acres of land in Lonavala, and three offices—amounting to 8,000 square feet in the prime business district of Nariman Point.

Finally, they relented and agreed to give me the money. The three-pronged approach worked and SSKI was saved. However, there was no business and we had astronomical salaries to pay.

After I repaid my corporate clients I had Rs 3–4 crore that I could use for business. But business was not forthcoming. I travelled to the USA, UK, Hong Kong and Singapore, requesting people to trust me and the firm. I had to convince them that I was a victim. Yes, I had made a mistake, but my mistake was exaggerated by the Marwari lobby. But nobody could understand that and neither business nor trust was forthcoming. I plunged into a very dark space.

The precarious financial situation was hampering the well-being of my wife and daughter, who was in grade VIII. My temper issues were not helping the situation and I decided that my wife and daughter would move to Ahmedabad, so that they would get the comfort of 'home' and much-needed emotional stability from my in-laws.

If you shared your problems with my father-in-law, you would come out realizing that your problems are minuscule compared to the problems of the world. He would make you see your issues from his prism and he would also shroud you in love and respect. He always said one thing: 'If the problem is larger than your ability to solve it, lay it at god's feet. He will solve it. And if he does not solve it, it is for your good whether it is in this life or the next.'

Kalpana and Ami left for Ahmedabad the next day. I was alone at home with my dog. There were two house helps to prepare my meals. There was no work at the office either. People would taunt me, by asking what was I up to when they knew I had no work. Most of my employees had left, but my CEOS—two of my best people—stood by me.

Once, when I was flying back to Bombay from the United States, I had a chance to meet with a technocrat who had been offered a telecom mobile licence for a few circles, including Mumbai.

His company's ADR (American Depository Receipts) was floated by a renowned US bank that had a prominent lady heading its investment banking division. The firm had failed to raise $150 million for the technocrat and his business was in desperate need of large-scale capital.

Frankly, I did not know what mobile telecom or ADR meant, but I told him confidently that I could raise money in eight days. However, it would have to be at a 20 to 25 per cent discount to the earlier proposed price. Back then, I did not even know what the price set by the foreign firm was. I had an intuition that this deal would not only save my potential clients' telecom business but also help me regain my lost reputation.

The promoter stated point-blank that I had ten days.

My clock was already ticking.

I was determined to stay true to my word and the first thing I did was to meet my CEO, an equity research analyst, and a brilliant mind from IIM Calcutta. He had several offers, but stayed true to SSKI as he had faith in me and the institution I was trying to build. I told him that this deal had to be done at any cost. If not, our firm would be wiped out from the face of the Earth. 'I have lost my family, all my business and assets. We must make the telecom deal happen, otherwise I am finished. You will get other jobs but my career will end prematurely.'

Next, I meticulously studied the newspaper reports on mobile telecom transactions. There was no Google in those days and I got all the newspapers and business magazines and read about the corporate venturing into a new-age business. Buried in one article, I read about a Washington-based fund that was interested in this transaction, but they found the pricing too high. I sourced the contact person of the fund and made a cold call, stating that I had the mandate for raising funds for the telecom company.

At the outset, the man on the other line refused point blank, saying that the technocrat in question was a tough guy and would not budge. I told him to leave it up to me and requested for a meeting. It was 10.30 p.m. in Mumbai. That very night, I left with my CEO at 1.30 a.m. on the British Airways flight, and we were in Washington by noon.

Like I said, I did not know anything about telecom or the number of subscribers, ARLI, spectrum, revenue license, etc. I only knew this was going to be a make-or-break deal for me.

The fund manager in Washington informed me that he had a consortium of investors that were willing to pick up $100 million at $7 per ADR, as opposed to the promoter's expectation of $10. I blurted out, 'You give me a leeway of $7.5. I am not asking for the impossible. Just 50 cents per piece and I assure you, I will get the deal done. I am an entrepreneur and I know how another entrepreneur's mind works. Secondly, I need the term sheet in twenty-four hours because I have a limited time frame mandate.'

My heart was pounding as I finished the sentence. After a brief silence, which felt like an eternity, the fund manager agreed with my condition of $7.5, as opposed to the promoter's expectation of $10.

I called the promoter in the morning, Indian time, and told him that I would be in Washington for a day as the term sheet was being prepared. Frankly, I had never seen a term sheet in my life and neither did I know what it stood for.

Then my CEO politely explained all the challenges we could face if we went through with this deal. But for me, it was not just a deal—it was a matter of survival. If this clicked, I would not only be out of debt but would able to catapult my business to the next level.

My CEO flew back and got down to work on the financial modelling. I started work on gaining knowledge about the cost of the airwaves, spectrum, etc. There is a lot to learn when one is doing a telecom deal. I used to call my CEO every night and badger him with telecom-related questions. After all, I had to appear smart. If the fund managers figured out that I was clueless, it was the end of the deal.

On the second day, I got a term sheet. The term sheet was marked at $7. I lost my cool. 'Why are you f***ing around with me? I told you I wanted it at $7.5, did I not?' I snapped.

He said, 'I am giving you a letter authorizing you to increase it to 7.5 dollars, if the promoter does not agree.'

I snatched the letter and took the first available flight back to India. En route, I called my CEO and asked him to join me in Bangalore, where our 'saviour' was based. After landing in Bombay, I took the next available flight to Bangalore. There was no time to waste.

At the outset, the promoter was shocked, but once he regained his bearings, he asked, 'But what is the proof that they will do it?'

I said, 'I have no proof. But the very fact that someone has spent time and legal fees on issuing this term sheet clearly shows their intent.'

Convincing the *promoter* was much tougher than convincing the *investor*. But I persisted—and met with success. That very evening, he signed on the dotted line.

I called up the fund manager. I told him briskly that the term sheet was on. Now, he and his team had to come to India, to take this deal forward. The man was chuffed as he was finally meeting the promoter to do India's first mobile telecom deal!

Very soon, the legal and commercial due diligence began. All of it was very new to me. My CEO and his colleagues handled this part along with the officials of the promoter's company. I could not complete the deal in seven days. But in two-and-half-months, we sealed a private placement of the first ADR placed by an Indian company in the overseas market!

The second company to do it was Infosys Technologies. We raised $100 million, which was around Rs 500 crore then! My fee was going to be Rs 15 crore! News of this deal flashed across newspapers. Several people at the foreign investment bank's office in India lost their jobs. Suddenly, I became the toast of the town.

Yet again, life was on an upswing. However, getting our fees from the promoter was an uphill task. I had to beg him for money that we were rightfully owed. One time, I even touched his feet, pleading, 'Sir, I am very loyal. Whenever you want, I am there. I am there for you, but please pay me my fees.' Eventually, he paid in two instalments.

And thus, I was able to repay all my debts! From the fees and selling surplus real estate, we moved to a rented premises.

I was an unsung hero. I had had a hard fall—a fine of Rs 76 lakh, suspension for seven days and no FII willing to give me any business. Then suddenly, I cracked a $100 million ADR deal, which a large foreign bank could not sell. I was on every headline between 1998 and 1999. The *Economic Times* had my photograph on the front page. The phoenix had risen from the ashes.

In the meantime, I started visiting my in-law's family home in Ahmedabad to spend time with my daughter. I would reach on Friday and leave on Monday. Over the weekend, I would help her with her studies. My daughter was going through a difficult time. She felt out of place, in a new school and environment. It was a school run by my mother-in-law. Ami was often asked why she was here when she was supposed to be in Mumbai. Children can be cruel at times, but over time, the love of her grandparents began to heal the cracks in her heart. Slowly, her eyes began to radiate the happiness that comes from emotional well-being and I could not have asked for more.

My family and business were back on track. But like always, I kept wondering, 'Will these good times last?'

7

Flying Higher

God turns you from one feeling to another and teaches by the meaning of opposites so that you will have two wings to fly not one.

—Rumi

1999–2005

In the case of the mobile telecom operating company, what was to be a $100 million fundraiser, skyrocketed to a $250 million transaction, comprising seven to eight investors and a mix of primary and secondary offerings! This was because we did multiple rounds of funding. Single-handedly, that one deal had revived SSKI. I could repay my debts, whether to the finance company of the largest industrial group or companies belonging to my wife's family. Debt-free, the firm was back in action!

I met one of the largest global American funds that wanted to take aggressive bets and asked me for a strategy. I showed them government companies that I thought were undervalued, but they did not want to do business with government companies. We introduced them to a pharmaceutical company and brokered a Rs 100 crore deal. Our fee was Rs 2.5 crore.

Then, another pharmaceutical company that had siphoned off money to invest in land parcels for its promoters approached us. We gave them ways and means to repay their flagship company. Unfortunately, they tied us up with Ketan Parekh (who eventually defaulted) for rigging up the share prices. The placement that was to be done at Rs 100 was done at a much higher price. I should have just walked out of the deal, but every investor wanted more and more of those shares, and I did Rs 150 crore of that placement.

I was then approached to do a placement of what is now a defunct IT company where a private equity fund wanted to exit. They then approached the same speculator to rig the prices. This IT company appointed a very experienced and charming CEO from a billion-dollar rival company. The CEO's personality was such that people began calling this company 'the next Infosys'. And everyone speedily invested in the company at rigged-up prices. It was a Rs 200 crore transaction. The close link between the two companies, and the now-defunct speculator/punter still active in the market much against SEBI directives, was evident. He would identify ten stocks, which were popular as K-10, that were his darlings. While I made my fees, he and the other speculators on the back of our placement information made a 100 times what my firm made. I suspect that some of the members of my sales and dealing team also participated in the 'bonanza'.

This way, I was doing one transaction after another. Then, the shareholders of a privately held broadcasting company wanted to do a placement of $125 million. They were not willing to sign the mandate letter, nor were they willing to give any information—there was nothing in writing. Moreover, they had a roster of preconditions, such as no guarantee for listing.

No investment banker was willing to entertain them. Except Shripal Morakhia.

I worked very hard. But although I took the responsibility, I did not know how such a deal would materialize.

A couple of nights later, I was in deep sleep, when the name of a fund that *could* make the deal happen came to my mind. I sat up, both jubilant and startled. It is never your intelligence that gives you the answers you need . . . it is the universe!

In the morning, I wrote an email to the fund manager, stating the placement of the broadcasting company. I got a prompt reply, stating that since the broadcaster's parent company was a revered client of the fund across the globe, they were more than happy to invest in the group company.

Next, I flew to Los Angeles and organized a call with the fund manager, the head of the broadcasting company based out of LA, and the CEO of the company based out of Mumbai. In less than two hours, the deal was done. It took me ten trips over three months to close the deal financially. In the process of money and shares changing hands, I learned two very important lessons:

1) Divide and rule to avoid the concentration of power. Although completing the deal was a super swift process, the financial closure drained me completely. It had to pass through various layers of management to get a sign-off, and then, finally, there were a lot of questions from their legal team to obtain the transaction documents. This required me to make ten trips.

2) Compliance is key. This was very different from my working style, where I regarded the given word as carrying more weight than the written one. (Little did I know that this misgiving would be the cause of my downfall.)

Today, I understand that business compliance is nothing but dharma. It is making sure that legally, all bases are covered, even if it involves a delay. Back then, I ignored it as I focused on the numbers and making sure the deal was closed.

After the final closure, I was approached by another fund manager of the same fund managing Japanese money, based out of Tokyo. I had met them during my trips to Los Angeles. This deal doubled to $250 million. Naturally, I made double the fees. The surge of deals continued. One of the most prestigious amongst them was a housing finance company deal for the American fund mentioned earlier. They had originally given the mandate to a Swiss broking company that could not procure shares from the secondary market. In the absence of alternatives, they came to me, and as always, the magic worked. I cracked an impressive deal, much to their surprise.

My good karma was on a roll. However, in my elation, I did not read between the lines. During the early days, when foreign investors made an entry into India, they mistrusted local brokers. There were rumours about me that I was front-running them. This was humbug. However, I learned that the members of my dealing room were possibly engaged in making a quick buck on the sly. Thus, I was not the first choice for the American fund. Moreover, the head of the housing finance company's disdain for me was apparent as he did not give me an appointment to meet him. I was thought of as a maverick, a wheeler-dealer and therefore, my firm and I never graduated to being a blue-blooded firm.

But I did not bother about the opinions of others. I did a deal for the then-largest retail chain, the largest music channel broadcasting company, and the first ten-pin bowling-based entertainment format with food and beverage that was promoted by a young man who is now the king of shopping malls!

This was my golden period from 1998 to 1999.

I was flush with enough funds to start a new venture. In SSKI, we were very good at dealing with large-scale institutional funds. But there was a potential market for retail investors that we had tapped in a small capacity. The CEO of our institutional business was keen on expanding into this market. The CEO of SSKI hand-picked four employees to start online trading. Thus, India's pioneering online trading platform, Share Khan, came into being.

I hosted a grand party to announce the launch of Share Khan. All brokers of the Bombay Stock Exchange were invited. I wanted to show that I had arrived. SSKI was a profitable business, and now I was launching India's first online trading platform with Share Khan. I was at the pinnacle of my success.

Share Khan was in troubled waters from the very beginning. I made it abundantly clear that my role was to be an investor and that the management team would be the promoters. Their entire business was based on the premise of the dot-com boom in the Western world, which had attracted billion-dollar investments. They spoke the right language, understood marketing and technology, and raised Rs 30 crore from three to four investors by diluting 35 per cent of the company. I was surprised that a start-up with no track record was able to raise this valuation.

This was the time when Amazon was in its nascent stage. We were in the first wave of the dot-com boom. Even someone selling sandwiches on the Internet would get a valuation of $250 million! That was the level of the craze. But at that time in India, there was just dial-in Internet, so Internet orders were not coming through in large numbers; 2G or anything of that sort was unheard of.

Despite raising the money, the 'promoters' did not have the right governance, due diligence and compliance. Sure, neither did I in SSKI, but I knew the balance sheet day in, day out and took responsibility for the revenues.

The biggest mistake I made in my life and something I utterly regret was that I did not set up compliance standards in any of my companies and too much power was concentrated in the hands of a few.

The top management of both companies thought that SSKI and Share Khan were running on their shoulders and that they were indispensable. The CEO I appointed in SSKI was aggressive and brought many deals to the company. It would offer the firm the revenue it desperately wanted. He, in turn, set up a system that would be able to manipulate the prices of the stock to his advantage and make 'n' times more revenue than what the fund made. In a matter of six months, he created a network of his own that would give him the deals. In nine out of ten cases, research would approve the deal and in turn, fees were made by SSKI while he made revenue from stock price manipulation. His system was foolproof.

Simultaneously, at Share Khan, the CEO began building his coterie. I told him that the COO he appointed was competent enough to drive the business. Worryingly, they had spent 90 per cent of the seed money without generating a single rupee of revenue.

I told him, 'Look we have come to a stage where there is a difference of opinion between us. I have invested Rs 4 crore in Share Khan. You have the choicest of investors like HBSC and Citi. I am happy to sell Share Khan to you—give me Rs 15 crore.'

But it was not to be. The next day, the bust in NASDAQ began. Even Amazon could have gone bust. Many companies like AOL, Amazon, etc., saw their share prices plummet and in a matter of three months, multiple companies went bust.

The financial shareholders of Share Khan were also shaken and they did not want to increase their investment in the company. My goal to make a quick exit could not see the light of day.

I was drawn again into a surgical strike. We had barely Rs 50 lakh of bank balance, while Rs 38.5 crore had been spent on marketing and creating their trading engine which had failed. I had no option but to fire ninety-five employees and rely on my brother-in-law who was made the CEO and two other employees—the head of technology and the head of compliance. The company had to survive on a limited bank balance and I made it abundantly clear that I would give no more than Rs 15 lakh. The size of the corporate office was reduced to just nine people.

The saddest part for me was that I had to fire the CEO of SSKI who had moved to Share Khan. He was like a brother to me and I had learned a lot from him. He meant a lot to me and that was the biggest loss that I mourn even today.

Another old guard, one of the few who regards me and SSKI as contributory to his professional growth was made head of investment banking. Around the same time, placements without adequate compliance started getting adversely affected.

Ketan Parekh too went bust at this time. All the stocks he supported went south and fell to approximately 25 per cent of their peak value. Pharma and IT companies lost a lot of value. Investors were upset with me and I was under tremendous pressure from a few fund managers to buy the unlisted stock and I had no option but to oblige. The retail pioneering company in its audited account wrote off old inventory and made a net loss, as opposed to the profits they had shown. The building in which the bowling company was housed fell and had to be shut down. The music broadcasting company promoters were clueless as to how to take the business forward. Some of the largest funds insisted that I buy back the shares of the retail company else they would have to stop doing business with me. I had no option but to agree.

Destiny is fickle. In a matter of a few weeks, from being a hero, I was now a zero. And just like that, without a warning, the downturn began . . .

The disgrace hit me hard. The broking business was affected and I had to do something.

I was fed up with myself—I had lost my name and reputation because of a few placements. I now decided to move from an active role in SSKI and decided that for both the companies, 50 per cent of the cash generated would accrue to employees and management as a bonus, and when I exited, one-third of the company would be distributed amongst the employees.

I wanted to be hands-off with Share Khan and SSKI, and focus on my next dream which was producing movies.

Growing up in the 1970s, I was under the spell of Hindi cinema. The first film I revelled in was *Jawani Deewani* starring Jaya Bhaduri and Randhir Kapoor. I was in school back then and song '*Jaane Jaa*' had enthralled the youth of India. With their foot-tapping music, picturesque Indian hill stations, and their larger-than-life heroes who would romance beautiful leading ladies, Hindi movies were exquisitely alluring. Who wasn't in awe of Amitabh Bachchan in those wonder years! The angry young man would fight against ruthless villains against all odds to bring home justice. The cult classic *Deewar* was a detour in that sense, but my heart went out to Vijay's (Bachchan's character in the movie) predicament. His unconditional love for his mother, as opposed to the nefarious life choices he was compelled to make . . . it was cinema at its finest. Out of the dark theatre, once back home, I would become Vijay. The mirror in my bedroom was witness to dialogue renditions from all the films in the 'angry young man's' repertoire.

With back-to-back debacles, investors had become anti-Shripal. This was in 2000. Revenues of both firms were affected because of the poor quality of placements and the losses incurred by retail investors on account of Ketan Parekh going bust. I had to arrange for some resources to keep the companies afloat.

A modicum of luck was still on my side and I got an opportunity to meet the larger-than-life founder and chief worker of a multi-billion-dollar conglomerate made in India. He had made his millions through dubious cheap funding, but when I met him, his company had interests in a variety of industries from media and films to airlines, real estate and sports. Apart from hosting glamorous film stars and cricketers, his opulent parties saw the presence of Indian politicians and foreign dignitaries.

My meeting with him was at the 250-acre luxury hill city he had built for the rich and the super-rich. I was delayed for the meeting by five hours—a car accident exacerbated by the infamous traffic leading up to the hill station had caused the criminal delay. I was extremely apologetic, but there was nothing I could have done. Right from my entry at the gate, every executive knew that I was to meet the big boss. One or two of them passed a snide remark about me having the audacity to make the great big boss wait.

Luckily, the big boss was empathetic to my delay. The media called him a cunning business tycoon, but I was mesmerized by his hypnotic aura. His charisma was inexplicable. I suspect that he must have studied tantric texts on how to control people. I was a seasoned businessman who could see through people and their agenda, but I fell under his spell.

Tea and snacks were brought in by six drop-dead gorgeous women. They hovered around him fussing over his tea. If flecks of jhalmuri flew off the spoon while he was having a bite, they would pick it up. They wiped dots of tea off his moustache. From the way they spoke and carried themselves, I could make out that these were well-educated women from good families.

The big boss ordered two of the women to show me the township. Before I left, I confessed to him frankly, '*Mujhe laga aap chor hain. Lekin aap kuch aur hi nikle. Aap ki soch aur drishti ki jitni prashansa karen voh kum hain.*' (I thought you were a thief, but you turned out to be something else altogether. I am impressed by your thinking and vision.)

A couple of months later, I was invited to his headquarters—a bustling heritage city in north India. The sprawling estate on which he lived included a cricket stadium, sports complex, movie theatre, health centre, fire station, petrol pump, 18-hole mini golf course, auditorium, and an open-air stage.

The guest room was grander than that of a seven-star hotel. I still remember the vast spread of dry fruit—I had no clue that there was such a vast variety available in nature.

At 11 a.m., we were called to the dining area. Without exaggeration, the dining table was half-a-mile-long. He had a microphone attached to the dining table. I requested him to fund my foray into feature films since he was in the business as well. His company had backed big-budget box office entertainers and legendary film-makers.

After agreeing readily, he asked me to attend a meeting organized for the newly-joined employees, which was scheduled a few hours later. What choice did I have but to comply?

Despite not wanting to, I went for the meeting. It was in his compound, which was as large as a football stadium. It was the induction ceremony of fresh recruits numbering about a 1,000 of this *desi* conglomerate.

My seat was in the first row. Everyone who entered had to say 'pranam'. Every five minutes, there was an update about the boss's whereabouts.

I distinctly remember there were seventeen such announcements, until his luxury sedan wheeled into the compound. All the 1,000 people stood up. The moment he got out of his car, everyone chanted, 'boss pranam', in practiced unison. He walked up to the stage and took a seat on a throne-like structure. Then strangely, for the next thirty minutes, there was pin-drop silence in the compound—the big boss did not say a word.

Then, the compere who had been making announcements before his arrival came up on stage. In complete servility, he asked, 'Pranam, sir . . . have we, albeit unknowingly, made any mistake to hurt you, sir?'

I wanted to laugh out loud. I whispered to my colleague, 'Imagine you rascals asking me when I enter the office—sir, have we done anything to piss you off?!'

My colleague softly replied, 'Just wait and watch, sir. The drama has just begun.'

Moments later, the big boss got up and said, '*Main bahut dukhi hoon. Aap ne mujhe pranaam kiya. Lekin aap Bharat Devi ko pranam karna bhool gaye.*' (I am very sad. You paid your obeisance to me. But you forgot the great Bharat Devi.)

The boss had created a deity called Bharat Devi. Her larger-than-life statue was the first that came into view when you entered any of his townships.

The compere and other seasoned employees shed tears, apologizing profusely for their transgression. The boss then took the mic and for the next hour-and-a-half, he held forth on the importance of the devi and how the principles of ancient Bharat are synonymous with the principles of the conglomerate. At that moment, I realized that he was a megalomaniac. The best way to get what I wanted was to feed his ego. I also realized something else. These people could and would build castles out of thin air. I, on the other hand, could not afford to do so.

When I returned to the guest house, I was asked to meet the boss again, this time without my colleagues. I touched his feet and told him that we had a lot to learn from him and this was all that it took to get generous funding. My unconditional obeisance paved the path for my movie business.

Yet another defunct company proved lucky for me. Six months previously, an Australian media company had made inroads into India, through another telecom company and Ketan Parekh. After the infamous speculator went bust, they lost interest in the Indian market. I took over their company, free of cost. It had receivables of Rs 25 crore, which would be mine if I collected the money. I succeeded in collecting a substantial portion of those receivables.

Back in the day, there used to be a channel called Doordarshan 2—the second metro channel of DD which was supposed to be in a joint venture with this Australian media company in which they had invested heavily. But when Parekh went bust, the government refused to renew the licence. The Australian media company wanted to exit the business. The receivables and blessings I received from the chief worker of India's first conglomerate and this defunct company helped me fund Share Khan and SSKI. This allowed me to take a backseat in the business and focus on producing movies.

As I said earlier, the biggest mistake I made was that I did not set up a strong compliance ethos. A company must have two separate sets of reporting authorities: one from a compliance perspective and one from a business perspective. Why, you ask? Because a business might not do well many times over. You might feel that it is doing well, but from a compliance perspective, it is not so. Of course, people are smart and they know how to hide these trails. However, for ethical business, I think that divide and rule is the best policy.

Thus, while Share Khan and SSKI grew, both companies became a personal money-making vehicle for its top employees.

SSKI Broking would get corporate clients; the dealers would buy shares in advance, and then make the placements based on news inputs which they would often fabricate. The irony was that out of the fourteen placements they did, all of them went bust. However, the firm to a lesser extent, and the key employees to a greater extent, benefitted from the transgression.

Since I used to travel frequently to London, the SSKI team spread the rumour that I had migrated for good. They wanted to project themselves as the supreme leaders of SSKI. One of my traders, a very loyal person, who had a solid background of working in a nationalized bank's mutual fund division said to me, '*Shripal, yeh jab phootenga toh aag ke babule niklenge. Tum bhi jal jaaoge.*' (Shripal, when this ball of fire explodes, you too, will get singed.)

Somehow, the CEOs and their coterie in both my companies felt they were larger than life and were not willing to accept any suggestions. My health was deteriorating, and I was diagnosed with a near-fatal ailment that resulted in many complications, physical, mental and emotional, which were the side effects of the medication. I remember I was resting when I got a frantic call from the bank. Our bankers had blocked our account, and the NSE and BSE had stopped us from trading. It was a crisis created due to a lack of compliance and a delay in the receipt of client funds. After a lot of cajoling and personal assurance, the blockade was removed. I was an exhausted man dealing with my illness and the trauma I faced from the bank.

This was how the afternoon unfolded: 2 p.m. was our deadline to make the payment. At 1.30 p.m., I was informed that the NSE had frozen our trading for non-payment of margin dues and HDFC was not supporting us. Weak and just out of the hospital, I dashed to the bank and pleaded with their credit risk manager to support us. At that time, the institutional and retail business was conducted under the same umbrella. Without their support, the FIIs would again strip us of our registration if they got a whiff of this. I was humiliated and gracefully accepted any barbs as it was a mistake made by our management. I promised that this was the last time I would be seeking their help and that I would never again approach them for help. They had extended support until now, helping us meet our short-term deficits, and we had taken this for granted. After 45 minutes of incessant pleading, the amount was released, saving me from further pain and embarrassment. It increased my resolve to exit the business.

Another reason to sell SSKI was continuous friction with my brother. If he procured a client, then he had to deal with the client. He would fight with me and abuse me in front of all the employees. He felt that I had taken a lot of money from the company when that was not the case. I was tired of the whole thing.

Now, he wanted to set up a pig iron company in Goa, etc. I said that we were not industrialists. He must have felt let down, especially after seeing that I was foraying into making movies, while he could do nothing without my consent.

People thought my net worth was Rs 2,000 crore. Yet again, I had zero personal bank balance except for the Rs 20 crore I had put in a trust account for the benefit of my wife and daughter, should something happen to me. Apart from this, I owned two flats in upmarket Altamount Road in Mumbai.

However, I was a disillusioned man. I had seen the corrupting nature of money and how low industrialists would stoop. Moreover, my health was giving me red flags. I knew I had to exit the business.

I felt I had lost a battle when I decided to give up both my businesses. But I did not have it in me to fight any further; I was tired.

8

My Exit from Financial Services and Learnings

Goodbyes are only for those who love with their eyes.

—Rumi

2003–2007

My decision to exit the business was final. I had no financial back-up to leave my family with in case anything untoward was to happen to me. Moreover, the stress of continued medical examination and the subsequent treatment was taking its toll on me. The continued spikes in my cortisol caused my body to bloat. My face had puffed up to the extent where people kept asking me if I was unwell.

The shareholders of Share Khan who were on the board were dissatisfied with the progress of the company. I told them that in the absence of additional resources, the only way we could survive was to find a new financial investor or a sell-out. A price of Rs 600 crore as the equity was the mutually agreed price.

In the past, I had quarrelled with the board, as they were against the issuance of warrants to the employees because, in addition to the salary, they were entitled to a variable pay of the cash generated. The warrants were 20 per cent of the fully diluted capital.

When we had been suspended from the stock exchange, the private equity fund that had invested in SSKI offered me their investment at a meagre rate. I used that as a pool for the Employee Stock Ownership Plan (ESOPs) in SSKI. I had never interfered in the cash-bonus allocation and had left it completely to the CEO to decide on the allocation of profits. Not surprisingly, in SSKI, the top two employees (the CEO and his acolyte, the head of research) accounted for 60-70 per cent of the variable pay, and in Share Khan, the top three accounted for 50 per cent of the variable pay. I never involved myself in the execution, as it was my policy to do so once I put my faith in the team. I had never taken a rupee of salary or bonus from the company.

I started the process and appointed a south-based investment banking firm for the sale of Share Khan. Before that, I tried to negotiate with the respective management team for a merger of SSKI and Share Khan, so that it would be a unique firm that catered to all the constituents of the market. However, both management teams could not see eye to eye.

The critical factor for the top five to six leaders of both organizations was the relative valuation of the two companies and the pool of ESOPs, and it created unnecessary skirmish and debate. I was mentally, emotionally and physically exhausted, and without putting up an argument, I simply aborted my attempt to merge the firms.

Sometimes, when a merger takes place, it is rendered useless by the egos of the top management and the cultures of the two organizations. That was something I had to think about. SSKI was entrepreneurial. With Share Khan, all power and processes were vested in the top three people and were very carefully funnelled down to other team members. It was much stricter in compliance than SSKI.

It was a very well-designed process from my perspective. In capital-constrained companies, I had to consider human resources as capital, but I never expected that greed would overtake the necessity to evaluate deals from the position of personal security.

For Share Khan, we were getting several offers from various reputed private equity funds. I asked my management team to take a lead as they were the surviving shareholders.

I had fixed the price at Rs 700 crore equity value and the decision was left to the surviving shareholders of Share Khan, i.e., the management team, to decide on new partners. All other private equity funds that had invested would also exit to make way for the new incumbent investor. After three months of negotiations on rights and obligations, they zeroed in on their new partner.

Once the new term sheet was received, they perused the surviving management team's rights and obligations. Now, those shareholders who had criticized the performance of the company, not only wanted to stay but also enhance their position in the company. I was not surprised. Such is the herd mentality of private equity investors. Very few people knew how to lead, though the situation has changed dramatically today.

I put my foot down and said, 'Nothing doing. You have stressed me out, and now you need to be out as agreed earlier.' There was one US-based private equity fund whose associate (partner) would come to Share Khan's office located at Phoenix Mill, where Starbucks had just opened. He would get his choice of coffee, come up to the office to gossip, and discuss everything except business.

This US fund came in the last round of funding, at an approximate valuation of Rs 400 crore. In a matter of two years, they were getting Rs 700 crore, but they harassed me to no end, especially when I was physically weak. They tried their level best to stay put. One day, as I was driving back after a medical procedure, I lost my cool and asked them to exit or else I would visit their head office and lodge a complaint against their behaviour. So they finally signed on the dotted line. This was the only hitch in the entire process. The statutory approvals did take time—much longer than expected, but once that was done, everything was relatively smooth.

However, SSKI proved to be challenging. My CEO wanted to buy the company with a crooked hedge fund for Rs 35 crore. He thought he was the mainstay of the company and had a grip on me. Taking advantage of my failing health, he tried to coerce me into deciding in his favour. He claimed that if he left, most of the organization would also go, and there would be no SSKI.

My body was in tremendous pain. I smiled at him and said, 'Let me think about it.' I then went to the head of the SSKI investment banking division, one of my first employees, and he told me that a leading infrastructure finance company was interested in investing. I asked him to get the term sheet. In a matter of one day, I was perusing a freshly minted term sheet at a value of multiple times that was offered by the broking head! The CEO was in a state of shock. There was no one he could express it to as I had left for the US.

This deal took time. At one point, the buyer doubted the compliances, and I initiated a thorough due diligence with a well-known accounting firm. Except for a small point, the other points were successfully ticked off. My head of broking, whose net worth now runs into thousands of crores, had at least not done anything foolish in our books. Finally, in May 2007, the deals were finalized. We received an amount of approximately Rs 500 crore for both ventures. I gave 50 per cent of the proceeds to my brother, who had doubts till the last moment whether I would part with my proceeds or not.

In those days, I had a hot temper, and we often had heated discussions. In every argument, I requested him to remember our past. When I was not well, he visited me twice, sounding extremely concerned. But once money exchanged hands, relations froze yet again. Now, he was dissatisfied as he felt short-changed here as well.

I breathed a sigh of relief when I concluded the transactions. No more of this tug-of-war with the employees who had all become larger entities than me. At this point, many in the outside world thought I was worth Rs 2,000 crore but all I had was the money recovered from the sale of my companies; a trust fund of Rs 20 crore; and 2,800 square feet of residential premises on Altamount Road.

SSKI and Share Khan were illuminating experiences. I learned about the psyche of top management, how the promoters of companies thought, how the small investors were treated, and the disparaging views of foreign institutional investors about Indian brokers.

The fund managers of foreign institutional investors had larger-than-life egos. Nothing made them happier than brokers massaging their fragile egos. In the initial years, I used to travel a lot to meet these investors and after each meeting, I wanted to throw up! I was sickened by the way investors behaved with us.

One fund manager based in Hong Kong would mock my Indian accent. Two fund managers from Singapore made me bend backward and dance to their ever-changing tunes before the business was rolled out from them. One fund manager, on hearing a baseless rumour, asked his dealing room to stop doing business with us. It was only after meetings in Mumbai and

NYC that the business commenced. In those days, we used to do management road shows with the investors. A Hong Kong-based fund manager in his late twenties/early thirties made it a precondition that I should not be present in the room. Many times, ideas would come from SSKI, but the execution and final order was done by someone else.

I experienced the most painful aspect of this business, as SSKI was the first Indian-origin broking firm and they were very suspicious of me since I was the face of the firm. One fund manager from Edinburgh accused me of financially aiding his associate during his stay in India. But all I had done was help the associate find a flat where he could stay with his wife and daughter for six months. Until 2000, I was the only prolific Indian broker and every second day, I would hear rumours about front-running my clients, or going bust. I still cannot understand how the two coexisted, as I was either honest and not making money, or I was front-running and making lots of money.

The year following our suspension was extremely painful. I became the butt of jokes and everyone in the system believed that I would not survive. However, they had to eat their words, when we had a windfall of lucrative deals and SSKI became a name to reckon with.

The foreign brokers were a different kettle of fish. They used a heavy American accent and tried to show their supremacy. Back in 1992–93, the head of a foreign broking house came to my office for a courtesy visit. The next day, my entire sales and dealing team was poached by his firm. Till 1997–98, senior employee turnover was very high, as my company became the poaching ground for foreign brokers, and later for fund managers as well. In my tenure, 352 senior employees left me. But those who remained had the last laugh, because they were handsomely compensated when I exited the firm.

One fund manager asked us to front-run him through the offices of our former foreign partners. One of them shared his office with my CEO after I sold the business. Everyone was a follower of Ketan Parekh and 90 per cent of the fund managers visiting India wanted to meet him. Another must-do activity for most of these fund managers was to visit Topaz dance bar near Novelty Cinema on Grant Road. This haunt was popular among the wealthy traders of the island city. They had abundant disposable cash to splurge on young girls dancing to foot-tapping Bollywood songs.

When employees start, they are extremely humble. As their efforts get appreciation from outside and their variable pay increases, their egos inflate. They begin to believe that they are the doers and they are the reason why the firm is making money. Furthermore, without them, the firm has no chance of surviving.

In SSKI, the turnover of employees was extremely high. Once, I hired the pharma head of research of an American broking house (that did not survive the 2007 crisis and was forced to merge with another American bank). He did nothing; absolutely nothing. He created a base for his hedge fund and left us. Another research analyst joined us. There was a woman in our sales team who, along with the research analyst, gave views contrary to that of the firm. She and the analyst even went to Hong Kong and dared to give contrarian views. Revolting against the company was unacceptable and my firm was financially capable of surviving without her business. The analyst and the saleswoman were instantly fired.

Keeping both firms afloat was an uphill task. In those days, there were bad deliveries of physical share certificates and at one point my entire capital was blocked in it. A huge team was specially created to sort the mess.

That was the time when SBI had come out with an initial public offer (IPO). The rules were vastly different then. People made applications under bogus names, as smaller applicants got a larger proportion of allotment of shares. There were hundreds and thousands of applicants with bogus names and fake signatures. When they sold the shares and these shares were registered by the custodians for transfer, the transfer was rejected. The custodian would hand over the certificates to us and we had to lodge it with the broker who delivered it. Though the rule was sixty days, many brokers violated the rules. We lost approximately Rs 2 crore in those days on bad deliveries, but ensured my clients were safeguarded and did not suffer. Yet the tag of being dishonest and shady would not leave me till I left the firm.

Except for a few, no one gave me any credit for my journey and experience. They thought they were the reason for the success of the two firms. I remember the day we were suspended. A relative who was working with me in SSKI came home with his wife and demanded that the amount due to him be cleared immediately as he did not know the future of the firm. My wife sold her jewellery and we paid him in a matter of two days. Ironically, the creditors in the market were more humane than my extended family members.

The third reason for my exit was the corporates. My first deal was with an IT company that became one of the largest in the country. However, its promoters got involved in a financial scam and it was sold to another IT company belonging to an automobile giant. This was in 1992–93 and they were going for a fundraiser. The promoter, who needed the money desperately, would offer illegal emoluments to me and my team members so that we would work harder.

A hospital chain promoter never decided on anything without consulting his daughter. A pharma company that had siphoned off money to buy real estate was able to regain its glory, after the promoter let go of his daughter.

Another promoter of an Indian media broadcasting company had a love-hate relationship with me. He was my role model as he was battling tremendous competition from foreign broadcasting channels making inroads into India. But most of the time, my suggestions would hurt his ego and he would threaten me with adverse consequences. Of course, I used to say sorry, only to make the same mistake again. My suggestions were simply that with an unknown auditor, there was not enough transparency in his balance sheet. Sadly, that increased after his involvement with Ketan Parekh.

The CEO of another broadcasting company whose placement I did was known to accept gratification openly and had a particular weakness for the opposite sex.

The promoter of a metal company based in London hired me to market the company and gave me shares instead of my fees. It was a great deal! His CFO, a blatantly dishonest man, is still a part of the company and had a stock broking license, was after my life to part with Rs 2 crore of my fees to him. And while the promoter knew about this, he said nothing.

As for the Andhra-based power-generating companies and their promoters we did placements for—the less said the better about their gold-gilded projects!

Finally, I must tell you the story of a media company whose ability to maintain relationships was top-notch. Everything else in terms of the performance of the company was rock-bottom. When animation was the trend, the company got involved in animation. If content for broadcasters was the flavour for the investors, the company became a content producer. When investors were shouting about intellectual property, the company went into movie production, and when Zee TV's (India's first private sector satellite broadcasting company promoted by the legendary Subhash Chandra) valuation reached sky-high, the company became a broadcaster.

The promoter was so good at getting money out of investors that every two to three years, there was a deal assured to SSKI from him. Most importantly, he was able to sell his media company to the largest global media major for a whopping valuation. Today, the global media major has shut down the entire operation of the company they acquired. This promoter is regarded as one of the greatest entrepreneurs in broadcast media and is a prominent philanthropist.

There are many such examples of promoters who behaved, acted, and spoke like Narayana Murthy of Infosys. But this was only at the time of fundraising. Many had scant regard for incoming shareholders and lacked the mettle it took to sustain a company for long.

The CFO of a major electronics company for whom the ex-chairman of the largest private bank and her husband were jailed, openly said that the group had one motive—'Operation Gora Luto' (fleece the foreign investor). This was prevalent at the time when research was relatively raw in India (until 2000) and operators had a say in the market.

For instance, one of our research analysts, a successful hedge fund manager today, wrote most of his reports at the Taj Chambers. It was an interview with the promoter that he passed off as a research report. Maybe he has learned from his mistakes today.

Out of the ten K10 stocks that were popular, seven have vanished into thin air. One has survived with the grace of the largest Indian telecom company. One pharma company was acquired by a Japanese company which in turn sold it to an Indian pharma major at a loss because of financial irregularities.

The last constituent was the private equity fund which spent millions in due diligence and had sleepless nights with a battery of lawyers in drawing up their agreements. But when it came to acting against a defaulting promoter, they were only interested in protecting themselves as opposed to punishing the erring individuals. The trend continues even today and fund managers are wary of suing the Indian promoters for wrongdoing.

Until 2020, investors were in awe of young and brash IIT/IIM entrepreneurs with their smooth language which most of the PEFs (private equity funds) could not understand. Their intricate business plans based on the infinite potential of the marketplace lured them to invest.

Today, making investments are based on the probability that x out of y investments will give them a great return and more than adequately make up for the loss of return and investments in the others.

When I see television shows on funding given by upstarts, who faced no or very few problems in their business lives or to other entrepreneurs at the 'venture' stage, I am filled with envy. Forget me. Even corporate giants like Tatas, Ambanis, Mafatlals and Birlas, have gone through their share of ups and downs. In India's capital market friendly environment (especially from 2015–2022), so many heroes were created. None of them are profitable yet, but that does not stop them from lecturing everyone on the art of making money and flashing cheques to potential investors, the same way that a client would flash money at a nautch girl.

I enjoyed the journey till it lasted and had no remorse or regret about selling the business. In every venture, I treated my management team and employees as partners. I always reiterated that my chief resource was my staff. People with money reward their shareholders, but I chose to reward my people. I primarily changed the ESOPs, bonuses, and salary structure of the industry.

Many of my employees grew bigger in life while I diminished bit by bit over time. There was the constant pressure of people leaving and the next deal not materializing and this played havoc with my mind, body and family life.

My first investment analyst told me a story about a company that would collect lemon peels from roadside lemonade sellers and convert the waste into lemon pickles. I was aghast to hear the story and shocked beyond words, when we got an order to buy the stocks of that company. I was so furious that the analyst understood that he was no longer required by my company. He resigned and became a mutual fund manager of a company that is defunct today—though he is a very rich man personally.

In my thirty-odd years of doing business, I developed the ability to see through any person and his objectives when associating with me. I have seen capital come, multiply, and even dissolve. There were times when no capital came in when it was most needed. I came from an era where the broking business did not get its due credit and by the time it did, I was an exhausted man.

9

Family Time

Love as much as you breathe

Love as long as you live.

—Rumi

2007–2014

As I sit back and recollect my life's journey, I can see that there have been umpteen ups and downs, but it was always my wife and daughter who kept me grounded. What I regret most today is the sacrifices they made. Their expectations of me were the bare minimum. I need not have spent so much time obsessing about building one business after another. When they required me most, I was never around for them. And despite that, they were always around when I needed them, no questions asked. I am grateful to god for their continued acceptance.

I have told you about Kalpana.

Let me speak now about Ami.

My daughter was born when I was three months short of turning twenty-four. She is and will be the most precious person to me. And yet I could not give her peace, even when she was in her mother's womb. The first ten years of her life were emotionally erratic, because of my financial and mental anxieties, and yet her love for me never diminished.

I still remember that she was all of five when I was down with pneumonia. It was my birthday and so she insisted on going with her ayah and buying gifts for me. It is the sweetest thing anyone has done for me. When I think about that moment, tears fill my eyes even today. Her sole concern was whether papa would like her gifts.

When the sun shone down on us, we had some very good times as a family. I would tell her stories and she would doze off to sleep, listening to them. The next day she would insist on hearing the rest of the story. We have grown up together and she has been more of a friend than a daughter. Despite all our ups and downs, the three of us—my daughter, wife and I were a close-knit troika.

During the two years that we were apart, my daughter went through mental turmoil. In the ninth grade, she was old enough to know that all was not well with me, yet too young to understand the complications of business. This was the period when my firm had been suspended from the Bombay Stock Exchange. But even though I was not financially stable, I ensured that we took vacations, and at least on one vacation, my mother would accompany the three of us. That resulted in fostering a solid bond between a grandmother and her grandchild. Apart from the three of us, we often went on holiday with my two cousin sisters and their families.

Incidentally, during the tragedy of 9/11, my daughter was an undergraduate studying in the US. Being artistically inclined, she pursued fashion and advertising. While she was there, I went at least fifteen times to New York, during her first year in college, just so that I was sure that she had a comfortable life there. My wife would often accompany me. I would go shopping for groceries and Kalpana would cook my daughter's favourite *ghar ka khana* (homemade food) like green moong dal, bhindi and rice. During this time, while Ami was in college, my wife and I travelled far and wide. The period between 2001–2006 was the best for the two of us as a couple. We were inseparable. Having seen the best things that money can buy, I must say one thing: there is no greater joy than conjugal bliss. I am eternally grateful to god and the universe for granting me this grace.

But duality is a way of life. Where there is happiness, sadness must exist. It was during this time that my sister was plagued by gangrene due to her high diabetes. She was in a coma for four to five days and one day, she woke up in the middle of the night, looking sparklingly fresh! There was an inexplicable aura around her. She then spoke to all of us in the family.

As she was recuperating in Bhatia Hospital, I decided that I would spend all my time with her. The fifteen days I spent by her side seemed to do her good. We got very close. I was glad to see that post-surgery, she seemed to be doing well. But, worryingly, she was under the illusion that her leg had gone for 'repair' and that she would get it back soon. I would divert her mind with food. Bhatia Hospital is a stone's throw away from the famous Swati Snacks, which offers the best vegetarian *chatpata* (spicy) snacks. I would tempt her with her favourite paanki. We talked about a lot of things in those days. One day, while I sat and chatted with her, she smiled at me, 'Shripal, you have become a good man now.'

That's when I knew that our relationship had resurrected.

Back then, I would stay with her in the hospital. One night, something woke me up and I checked the time. It was 2.30 a.m. The private nurse had dozed off. Something prodded me to check on my sister. I went to her room. She was lying there peacefully, but she was still, so still that she did not respond to the sound of my voice calling her name . . . and that was when I realized that I had lost her forever.

It was the most heartbreaking moment of my life. I had not been able to gauge her mental disorder when we were young. It was only fifteen years later that we knew what it was—yet my mother had refused to medicate her. My sister was brilliant and beautiful and had a PhD in French literature. When her disorder was at a nascent stage, she worked at TELCO. It was the most blatant display of karma that I witnessed—she had everything but could enjoy nothing.

Grief opens doors to a new source of happiness . . . albeit temporarily.

For me, my daughter's graduation was the peak of my happiness as a father. I felt good about giving my daughter a better life in the US. I was able to educate her without any struggle. She had financial support as well as the luxuries that I had not had when I was a student in the US. She worked hard, did not take her privileges for granted, and studied diligently. We were so chuffed to see her graduate with impressive credentials!

The biggest tragedy of my life was the little time I spent with her after her eighth grade. She was under the care of her grandparents during the ninth and tenth grades. I travelled extensively when she was in junior college and it was only when she went to the US for six years that we bonded.

After graduation, she worked for two years in the US. However, she was back home, just before my sister's death. Once the sale of SSKI and Share Khan were done, we started looking for a prince for my Ami. A few months later, we met her prospective groom. Despite meeting through an arranged marriage, my daughter and prospective son-in-law got along effortlessly.

We hosted the wedding at Amby Valley as it had to be a grand and luxurious affair. At the time, I was flush with funds. The wedding ceremony was so serene that I thought I was in heaven. There was pin-drop silence during the rituals because after chanting the Sanskrit mantras, the wedding pandit would explain their meaning and importance in Gujarati. Time stood still as everyone paid attention to the wedding ceremony.

During the ceremony, I had an epiphany: a daughter is always yours and yet never yours 100 per cent. She continues to nurture you and take care of you in your old age, but once she is married, she has a new set of responsibilities. The entire dynamic changes. It is heartbreaking, but that is the reality of life. Marriage is a happy occasion tinged with sorrow and nostalgia. The separation from one's daughter haunts you especially when one has grown up as friends.

My daughter was the harbinger of all the goodness that came into my life. I mellowed down and became a better human being after I held her for the first time. She brought my wife and me closer as a family. Just before her marriage, I was diagnosed with depression and was disturbed by the thought that her room would always remain empty. The agony of our prospective separation made me so anxious and depressed that I was prescribed allopathic medication to alleviate the anxiety. My medication continues to date.

Many had predicted that my financial downfall would begin after my daughter's marriage. I was a strong believer in astrology. When times are good, everything the astrologer (and I had a panel of them) predicts comes true. However, during bad times, nothing they say makes sense. They recommend pujas and *havans*. I fell victim to this money-making racket. I was advised to put an impression of my new-born daughter's feet in the money safe and I did so. But eventually, only karma dictates the outcome of one's life. The repercussions of bad karma cannot be avoided by lighting a diya or someone else reciting the mantras.

My daughter had a successful fashion business. She opened a store named Creo at Kemps Corner. Four years into her marriage, we were blessed with two beautiful granddaughters. The love for one's grandchildren is inexplicable; it can only be experienced.

During the period I lost my sister, my family had increased as three more members joined the fold: my son-in-law and two beautiful granddaughters. My mother was ninety-six-years-old at the time of writing this book, but she has the steely nerve to stay independent. God doesn't make people like her any longer. The loss of my mother-in-law and father-in-law was immense as I had always seen them as beings akin to god. The Webster Dictionary defines godliness as a religious life/a careful observance of religious duties, born from the love of divine characters and commands. Kalpana's parents were the embodiment of godliness.

As for me, over the years I have aged. I am an old man, hunchbacked, I am losing my teeth and becoming heavier . . . but what keeps me alive is family. Death is the greatest tragedy of life and the connections of the soul are cut short by its eventuality. Another harsh reality is that connections within the family are often transactional. Your sacrifices for them mean nothing. Yet there are others, like my cousin—the orthopaedic surgeon, and his wife; my cousin sister, and brother-in-law, who have been and will continue to remain the pillars of our lives.

Life constantly evolves, relationships change, and sometimes communication stops for the strangest reasons. You mean nothing to people you thought you were close to, and have seen as children, once they become successful.

But life goes on. We must go through our karmas. Loving, fighting, hugging, and hurting is what living is all about, after all.

10

My Film Production Business

Out beyond ideas of wrong doing and right doing, there is a field.
I will meet you there.

—Rumi

2000–2010

If I had an option in life, I would love to be an actor. But I am a realist, and given my looks and a hunched back, I gave the thought a pass.

When my daughter was growing up, I wrote a story and then commissioned a well-known and respected screenwriter to write a screenplay for its onscreen adaptation. The story revolved around god ordering his demigods to change the environment of an unhappy family in which the children were suffering. Like all brilliant stories, it had universal appeal and is as relevant today as it was in the late 1980s. I knew how much my family had sacrificed to fulfil my aspirations.

Decades later, after taking a backseat from SSKI, my passion for cinema was rekindled. But this time it was not acting that

I was keen on. I brainstormed with my former media analyst at the broking firm and we came up with the idea of small-budget films without stars but very high on narrative. The story and screenplay would be the main attraction for footfalls in the theatre. Thus, I-Dream Production, a boutique studio, was born to make high-quality content at a low cost. No film of ours was to exceed a budget of Rs 7 crore.

16 December, released in 2002 marked our foray on the celluloid screen: an action thriller with an ensemble cast with model and actor Milind Soman at its helm. The film did decently well at the box office and established I-Dream as a production house to watch in the Indian market.

But all that glitters is not gold. The path to making this film was rife with friction. Just as we were first-time producers, the director who was an advertising film-maker, was also making his debut in the long-format narrative.

Initially, he shot a rather clunky climax and when I saw it on the edit table, I was aghast. I put my foot down and insisted on several other options for the climax. Finally, we rewrote and reshot the climax. In my view, the director had taken shortcuts and his primary aim was to make money while the film came second. After much creative meddling, we finally had a film that we were proud to release. But on the flip side, the film had gone way over its budget—from Rs 3.5 crore it shot up to Rs 6 crore. We marketed the film aggressively. Back then, it was the first non-star cast film to be marketed with such vigour. Luckily, it turned out to be a theatrical success. However, a wrong TV deal on account of lack of experience led to financial losses. Since it was our first film, I took it as a learning and did not dwell on the losses as I wanted to be associated with more films.

That is how we became distributors for much-acclaimed films like *Monsoon Wedding, Bend It Like Beckham* and *Bollywood Hollywood*. We attempted unique marketing strategies to promote the films, especially *Monsoon Wedding* and *Bend It Like Beckham.*

For *Monsoon Wedding*, the entire cast and crew danced in a *baraat* starting from the iconic Taj Mahal Hotel to Regal Cinema for its premiere. The cream of the corporate world attended the screening—no one was marketing Bollywood films like we were.

Bend It Like Beckham was less difficult to market as it had been released around the soccer World Cup. The director's next film *Bride and Prejudice* was supposed to be made on a budget of $2 million, but after the success of *Bend It Like Beckham*, she increased the budget to $8 million and so we parted ways.

I did not have much interaction with Deepa Mehta though her film *Hollywood Bollywood* made a mark on the audience. Its song *Rang Rang Mein* was a chartbuster for many years after the release of the film.

These three movies helped us gain a firm footing in the film industry. While we did not make too much money, I-Dream became an established brand. When people switched on their TV sets (back then YouTube and social media were not prevalent) and saw our trailers, they would know it was an I-Dream production. We were on track.

Next, I launched a family film with songs, special effects, and a known name—Javed Jaffrey. The story was a combination of the Gujarati folk story *Bakasur* and *Gulliver's Travels*. The film took three years to make because of the heavy use of VFX and had a whopping 63 minutes of special effects—more than any other film at that time. Several times, I wanted to shelve the film but did not have the heart to do so. Eventually, I made sure *Jajantaram Mamantaram*, or J2M2 as I fondly call it, saw the light of day.

Meanwhile, Hrithik Roshan's *Krrish* was due for release, and we only had a two-week window. J2M2 was one of the few films that was close to my heart. A timeless story, it was loved by children. It had a long life on television, even after the theatrical buzz died down. Its director, lead actor, and supporting staff, coupled with excellent music and special effects, made it my all-time favourite film team. If I had to make this film all over again, I would bear ten times more pain, because it was a product of the sheer hard work and the passion of all 300 members of the crew and cast.

We made a spate of films. Out of those, one came with the company I had acquired from a joint venture with Ketan Parekh, HFCL, and Kerry Packer. The film was *Agni Varsha*. When I first saw it, I thought to myself, '*Aai shapath*, this is I-Dream's *Lagaan*.' It was so beautifully picturized. Raveena Tandon had never looked more ravishing than she did in this film. I genuinely thought that I-Dream had hit the bull's eye. But to my utter disappointment, it turned out to be a dud at the box office and today, it's available on YouTube.

My CEO said that it was his turn to commission a commercial film. Thus, *Samay* was greenlit and was made by a technically sound ad film-maker. The stunning Sushmita Sen looked her part as a razor-sharp police officer. But a weak script undid the film, and it was a box-office failure.

I thought that if people were experimenting on my hard-earned money, why could I not make a film myself? Why didn't I put all my focus and energy to truly grasp the craft of film-making? In those days, the copyright laws were not as stringent as they are today. I was fascinated by horror films, especially those from the Far East. They were getting remade even in Hollywood. I was exploring the possibility of remaking *The Eye*, directed by the Pang Brothers, when Soni Razdan was also planning on remaking the same under the Vishesh Films banner.

Along with a freelance writer, I rewrote the entire second half and tried to Indianize it as much as possible. On the sets, the cinematographer wanted to have his way all the time and it took me fifteen days to break his hold. He also made the most blatant use of state-of-the-art cameras, equipment, and lights, all at my expense. One day, I snapped and fired him after the shift was over.

As a director and producer, I was hands-on with *Naina,* as the movie came to be called, and found film-making a fascinating experience. Whether it was a glass particle piercing someone's eye, a train to be set on fire, or an entire petrol pump to be blown up—the sheer possibility of creating magic on screen was an adrenaline rush.

Many believed that I was merely a namesake director and that someone else had ghost-directed the film. Vicious rumours were spread about me, but I was undeterred. I was enjoying the learning process and I could not have asked for an actress more patient than Urmila Matondkar. I was in awe of her punctuality, patience and professionalism and we both took great pains to take the movie to the next level.

Once I saw the final edit, I realized my mistakes and promised myself that if I ever made a horror film again, I would not repeat these errors. The horror scenes were all packed in the first half. Moreover, it was during the filming of horror scenes that I realized I did not have adequate shots for the build-up of horror. The second half was an emotional drama. The movie opened very well, thanks to a series of trailers that were released on TV channels and Urmila Matondkar's star power added to the attraction. We also got publicity from a suit filed by the All-India Ophthalmological Society asking for a ban on the film. After all any publicity, whether positive or negative, is good publicity.

Naina opened to packed theatres on Friday and the first day collections were impressive, said the film trade pundits. The film gained word-of-mouth momentum right from the first day of the first show. Incidentally, Soni Razdan's version of *The Eye*—*Nazar* was released on the same day as *Naina*. Surprisingly, its reviews were not great and it carried a three-star rating!

Unfortunately, during the weekend, there was a bomb blast in a cinema hall showing a Sunny Deol film. As a result, shows across theatres were cancelled. *Naina*, the film, could not recover from the setback. A week later, *Bunty Aur Babli* was released.

During the making of *Jajantaram Mamantaram* and *Naina*, I found two great teachers who were versatile and patient enough to teach me the craft.

One of them, Pankaj Advani, passed away at a very young age. A national award-winning film-maker, he was not only a genius but generous as well. He helped me immensely when it came to both films, especially on the edit table.

The other was Biju—a genius when it came to visual effects. I am truly blessed to have learned the power of cinema from these two gifted gentlemen. They made anything seem possible. For example, Pankaj took a terribly shot scene and made it look great; I gave him an incomplete film and he made it look comprehensive. Biju, the VFX advisor to the best talent in the industry, took a hiatus post 2010. He went to Singapore to teach and now makes audio-visual installations for world-class museums. I was to work with him on another project based on Sanatan Dharma. Unfortunately, the project could not see the light of day.

Another friendship I would cherish in my film-making journey was with bureaucrat, Sanjay Patil. One day, he told me that he had a script that would win all the National Awards. He was a simple man and I knew that he wasn't someone to make tall claims randomly.

My intuition kicked in and I invested my time and effort into his Marathi feature film, *Jogwa*. True to his word, the film won eight National Awards and is now a cult classic. However,

I must admit that I had had enough of movies by then, and the idea of opening a state-of-the-art gaming centre held great fascination. I could not provide the film with adequate resources for a theatrical release, so most viewers saw it on TV.

My reason for losing interest in the movie business was because of some of the film-makers I met.

In my view, the director of *Straight* messed up a good comedy despite her best intentions and good actors were wasted under bad direction.

There was another interesting movie we had decided to make with Robbie Grewal's* brother. It was the worst first cut I had ever seen and an actor of Paresh Rawal's stature was entirely wasted in a film shot on locations near Bhopal.

Tired of back-to-back film debacles, I decided to wield the magic one last time. When I made *Naina*, I was accused of making a copy. So this time, I decided to write and direct an original sex-comedy. When my daughter saw the film with her friends, she asked me if I was on dope. The film was called *The Pinocchio Effect*, and I couldn't market it because I fell gravely ill during the making of the movie. However, for those who would like to see it, it's available on YouTube.

Despite the setbacks, I do not regret my film-making journey. From the spot boy and the light man to the director, it is teamwork at the end of the day. Sure, the inflated egos of successful people at the top run amok. I was in the eye of the storm due to ego clashes on the sets of *King of Bollywood*. The troika of the director, the lead actor, and the leading lady made

---

* Robbie Grewal was one of the founders of Red Ice Productions, a leading production house creating advertising commercials. Robbie had directed *Samay*, starring Sushmita Sen, for I-Dream Productions.

my life hell. As if that were not enough, there was an income tax raid on our stockbroking offices.

Two famous superstars had been given advances by I-Dream—Rs 50 lakh and Rs 25 lakh, respectively. It was made clear to them that if the script was not satisfactory, the money would be returned. The younger superstar of the two sent me a message saying—'Please consider that your money is with the RBI. It is yours when you want.' After sending me a legal notice, one crorepati actor returned 80 per cent of the amount, but the younger actor has yet to refund the amount.

Trust me, I have never seen so much lust for money (a lust greater than that for sex!) as I have seen in Bollywood. This greed was not even in the stock market, where profits are the only determining factor.

Before I end this chapter, I would like to tell you one last story. I was by myself for four to five days once in the 40,000 square feet office of a defunct company in Los Angeles.

At that time, I imagined a scenario where disgruntled employees would haunt the person who had fired them. I added a boss on prescription drugs for mental disorders on account of stress and depression, for good measure. In a matter of two hours, I wrote a script titled, *Fired*. I wanted to make the film in 3D, but we could not lay our hands on the right equipment. We finished the film and sold it to a distributor. Unfortunately, it never saw the light of day.

Today, I wish I had started I-Dream fifteen years later. Now is the best time for films that are high on content and demand talented actors instead of stars.

11

My New Business Ventures

Don't be satisfied with stories, how things have gone with others.
Unfold your own myth.

—Rumi

2008–2012

After my exit from SSKI and Share Khan, the message from god and the universe was clear—*Take it easy. You now have a fresh lease of life. Instead of looking outward, take time out and look within yourself. There is a whole new world to be discovered.* But the illusion of the material world—maya—was so alluring that I failed to stop. After all, it is hard for us mortal beings not to be in the limelight.

Though my film business only drew a lukewarm response, I still had red-hot ambition burning within me. I wanted to be the Walt Disney of India. Just as he created characters and built theme parks and movie studios around them, I believed our history and the Puranas were rich in content and waiting to be explored. I felt that the faith of a billion people could not be wrong. Our mythological figures possessed greater physical prowess and unique spiritual strength compared to those in Marvel and DC Comics.

In the case of Marvel/DC, there is a need to establish the character and its context and surroundings. However, since Indian mythology is so entrenched in our culture and in the minds of a billion Hindus, Indian characters are revered by us all. The spiritual connections that Indians have with gods and demigods and the stories around them embody creative imagination and fantastic storytelling. They were fertile grounds for creating an integrated studio experience.

It was with this conviction that I signed the deal for the acquisition of Amar Chitra Katha, the well-known comic book publisher, whose titles were largely based on Indian mythology and history. Wanting to convert it into a holistic 360-degree media company, I leased a 25-acre plot in the now defunct Hindustan Construction Limited-promoted hill city, Lavasa. A Canadian specialist architectural firm was appointed to design the Sanathan Sanskar Park—a project that would show our gods as the ultimate superheroes.

Every day, I dreamed of the stories that could be a part of Sanathan Sanstha Park: Lord Shankar's Tripura; Bhagwan Shree Krishna's battle against asuras; the journey of Prabhu Shree Ram; the evolution of Mathematics and various branches of Science for which our Vedas and Upanishads got no credit. I was now building a team for the evolution of Amar Chitra Katha as a physical and digital media company and even appointed an ex-McKinsey director from NYC who shared my grand vision for ACK.

As soon as the organization developed, we received news of a ban on any construction in Lavasa. Time, energy, and most importantly, Rs 5 crore, had been invested in the preliminary legwork. We had to think on our feet and come up with another plan. Soon we started the process of digitizing the ACK library while simultaneously pushing the sale of books through more traditional channels. It was tough at the time because retail book sales were not well-organized and receivables would keep on mounting. The ACK management team recommended buying the biggest book distribution company, owned by the same family that owned Amar Chitra Katha. Thus, to increase sales of ACK, we decided to buy India Book House. It was an ill-fated decision, because along with IBH, we also took over its problems as collateral damage.

In the meantime, I was trying other options for land parcels, while keeping myself abreast with all emerging and existing audiovisuals, rides, and sports technology. I went to the extent of pitching the idea of Sanathan Park to Sentosa Island in Singapore as the vast majority of tourists were from India. In our country, the hassles associated with buying agricultural land, consolidating it, and finally converting it for theme park usage is an arduous uphill task. It is something that only powerful politicians and those with unaccounted money can handle. It was not my cup of tea.

During this period, I had the good fortune of being in the constant company of Anant Pai or 'Uncle Pai', as he was known, the founding editor of Amar Chitra Katha and Tinkle. In my opinion, this gentleman should have been accorded the Bharat Ratna, for it is only because of him that generations of Indians know our gods, goddesses, warriors, saints and freedom fighters. For every frame of an Amar Chitra Katha comic, he knew the Sanskrit shloka behind it. He was a deep well of knowledge and only knew how to give. He never asked me or the previous owners for anything. All he wanted was ACK to fly high. When we took over the company we increased his salary—but frankly— no increments would do justice to this national treasure.

It is unfortunate that despite our efforts, my team and I could not bring back the glory of ACK. Again, I was ahead of the time. It was like a curse that continued to pursue me wherever I went. In this case, I was hampered by the lack of a distribution channel and the supremacy of a handful of strong national and regional distributors who put ACK under their thumb.

For me, the saddest moment was when, after twenty-five years, ACK published a new title—*Mother Teresa*. It was launched at the same time as a much-anticipated book from the Harry Potter series. We went all out with publicity to raise awareness for the launch of *Mother Teresa*. Unfortunately, it paled in comparison to the excitement surrounding the Harry Potter series.

Despite all these efforts, the growth was negligible. A private equity fund, promoted by the scion of the Dabur family, took one-and-a-half-years to invest less than Rs 20 crore in the company. Six months later, the former retail tycoon, Kishore Biyani, picked up a 25 per cent stake in the company.

I was constantly harping to anyone who would listen that unless we took a holistic view of the brand we were doomed. It was time that a company promoted by me went public. But there was no way that a Rs 25 crore company could go public. Worse still, we could not attract a single financial or strategic investor. Both Star and Zee TV turned down the proposal. The shareholders were indifferent to the slow pace. My financial investor from the Dabur family was basking in the glory of his father-in-law, Lalit Modi, who had given the digital rights of IPL for free.

Suffocated by this snail's pace, I decided to sell my stake to Biyani. His company, in which he had made investments in various brands, had just gone public. I accepted a cash deal with the understanding that I would invest the proceeds of the sale in his stock, so that his leveraging went down. Those were days when he had started accumulating large debts at his personal and operating company levels. The IPO had bombed badly, and he had to borrow aggressively to ensure that the issue was subscribed. Thus, the company had money, but he was financially substantially leveraged.

He honoured his side of the commitment, but I did not stand by mine. The parting was very acrimonious to the extent that they paid me 18 per cent less than what was agreed upon. It was one of the saddest decisions of my life, but I was helpless to do anything else. Why, you ask?

Well, as I wrote earlier, I had faith in Amar Chitra Katha. Unfortunately, we developed a top-heavy organization that was unable to increase sales. I did not foresee that direct-to-consumer sales would become so well established in less than a decade. None of the other shareholders shared my vision. I initially planned to invest Rs 20 crore, but the amount kept increasing and eventually reached a staggering figure of Rs 46 crore. After three years of hard work, I barely managed to recover the principal amount. I failed to learn from my mistakes at SSKI. The CEO took 25 per cent upfront in ESOPs. The challenges unnerved the management team, which began making one mistake after another. When the mistakes piled up, they jumped to other ventures. Within six months, the CEO started Scroll, and the COO launched Urban Ladder. Although they did provide ACK with a new CEO, my zeal and enthusiasm had already faded. Moreover, the unfortunate demise of Uncle Pai shattered me and I was a nervous wreck.

Around this time, I also decided to stop the movie business and give it lock, stock, and barrel to the then CEO of I-Dream. I had also invested Rs 35 crore in a bungalow in Lonavala. Another Rs 20 crore had gone into a duplex flat at Lodha Bellissimo in Mahalaxmi, Mumbai, and Rs 45 crore in disputed lands in Maharashtra, which were difficult to sell in the short run.

In addition, a further strain on my liquidity was on account of a collection of Lord Ganesha by master artists as well as upcoming artists that I had commissioned. I met two master artists of the older generations, one in Dubai, and the other in France, for commissioned works of art. In less than nine months, I collected 100 pieces of art showcasing Lord Ganesha. That acquisition cost was approximately Rs 22 crore.

However, the biggest cause of my distress was a Rs 61 crore investment in a telecom venture that did not take off.

Despite the odds and stiff competition from the largest Indian company, the company was revived by a professional team, and we got a bid that could have returned my entire investment. However, for reasons beyond my control, a sale did not materialize. My bad times had begun and I was under immense stress. I would have to write off Rs 71 crore of my investment or 65 per cent of the amount I received on the sale of an 18 per cent stake in Share Khan.

This augmented my anxiety about the dwindling fortunes. About 75 per cent of my cash reserves had petered out, of which 50 per cent were in the telecom venture, which I knew I would never see the light of day. My body reacted violently against the inhuman pressure. Soon I had a severe cardiac issue and I had to have a pacemaker put in.

Days later, I was diagnosed with atypical Parkinson's Disease. My biggest strength was the power to convince people. Now, I had lost the power of speech; my speech was incoherent.

Life had to go on, and I did not tell my family about the near-crisis situation that I was in. I turned to my last investment. Back then, Google had acquired YouTube. The latter was a content hub, and those who were providing content were making good money. I saw an opportunity on YouTube.

A very young team was hired under the leadership of my ex-colleagues of the film company, I- Dream. The company started with content available from freelancers in Bollywood as well as from Hollywood etc., and it was posted on the company's website and on YouTube. We went through many iterations and finally decided that our niche would be children's content. We scrapped our ownership channel to focus on YouTube because by then, the company had ideas for marketing content on it. To enhance our reach, we also collaborated with freelancers and influencers who could make the video viral in a few demographics.

With an exceptional singer on board, we began with nursery rhymes. The singer had an international-quality voice. As a result, we could head down and beat a lot of local channels who had an early mover's advantage over us. Thanks to astute marketing, within a year, North America became our number one market. It was obvious that to succeed, we had to have the USA as our market. Then, Jio was nowhere on the scene. The company did a few more skits for children, but nursery rhymes were our forte. We got strong traction. I visited one seminar on YouTube in the US, and our brand was recognized immediately by those present. I told the CEO that the time was ripe for me to exit and for the company to move to safer hands.

My life was an open book, and everyone knew my financial position. My CEO was supportive of my decisions, and though we appointed one of the four big accounting firms as the bankers for the deal, the buyer was identified by my CEO. The financial and legal due diligence was completed in four weeks and we agreed to sell my stake of 75 per cent at a fully diluted equity valuation of $24 million. The legal documentation commenced. The deal was with a Canadian subsidiary of a large German media conglomerate and I was very happy that just like my other two ventures this one had also found a good home.

We waited endlessly for the documentation. Time was running out as I had made some financial commitments, one of them being statutory. I was anxious about my depleting cash balance. The CEO of the Canadian firm (who was Iranian by birth) was never available. The people in Canada and Belgium, from where we were supposed to be receiving the transaction documents, had no clue as to what was happening. They had done their job, given the documents to the CEO and she was sitting on them. Then twelve days later, out of the blue, she called me and said that the board had rejected the deal on grounds of 'high valuation'. We argued and I told her this was not the behaviour expected of a reputed company. We agreed to meet the following week in Belgium, where the person she was reporting to was based. It was apparent that she had gotten a whiff from somewhere about my dire financial status. (This is the price that you pay for being transparent.) The other reason could be that she realized that she was buying a company that was based on the viewership of twenty songs.

With my CEO, chief creative officer and investment banker, I went to Belgium to meet the proposed buyer who was playing a cat-and-mouse game. I was desperate to sell the company. My dwindling cash balance, investments in hard-to-sell immovable assets, houses for personal use, and above all, losses in the telecom venture had made me extremely vulnerable. Initially, the discussion was not going anywhere, and there were arguments on trivial matters. They wanted to tire me out. They did not know that I was already fatigued and had come to close the deal. Finally, the Iranian CEO spelled out that the new valuation was down by 50 per cent of the previously agreed value of $12 million. It was evident that the buyer was playing dirty tricks to short-change me.

I was a cauldron of despair and heartbreak. Now, the mechanisms to set my financials right would be short by $10 million. They knew I would budge, after all, my body language was that of a man who had lost. I finally agreed. The deal gave me respite but not the relief I had desired.

I looked back at all the years of hard work and my business ventures—SSKI, Share Khan, I-Dream, ACK and now YoBoHo. For some strange reason, I was never able to obtain optimum or next-to-optimum value. Just three months after the Share Khan deal, it did a round of funding at 2.7 times the value it had been sold at.

I was personally making Rs 50 lakh a month and it was a princely amount apart from my properties and investments. Instead of climbing higher and higher, I should have just stopped. After all, I had a wife and child to look after and there was more than enough to lead a luxurious life. I could have focused on the charities I was sponsoring and my inner voice was softly nudging me in that direction. But listening to your ego instead of that inner voice, or subtle signs from god, comes at a price. And what a price I paid!

12

The Birth of Smaaash—India and USA

Don't wait any longer, dive into the ocean. Leave and let the sea be you.

—Rumi

2010–2016

The failure of the telecom venture and the renegotiation of the price of the digital venture shattered me to the extent that it took a toll on my health. I now had a pacemaker in my heart and atypical Parkinson's had affected my hand and impaired my speech. To top it all, I was 60 per cent down on my original wealth. But, not one to cower down and, against all odds, I decided to go in for the final kill.

My motivation came from Harvard psychology professor, Stuart Brown, who spoke on the importance of 'play' in developing a high emotional quotient as well as bonding. Dr Brown had dedicated most of his career to the study of non-competitive activity games and how they positively impacted mental and physical health. According to him, the lack of play resulted in depression and anxiety.*

He conducted studies on various successful and unsuccessful people, including serial killers and proved that people who made bad lifestyle choices like alcoholism or drug addiction had an absence of play in their lives.

As a father, I had not given enough time to my daughter. Now, I had been blessed with two adorable granddaughters. My mind was ticking. How could I make a group of friends or family play in a manner where there was no fear of losing? In an age where we add 'friends' to our social media via our phones, there was no concept of friends physically grouping to *play* just for fun.

Not anymore.

Clubs were elitist and out of reach. The lack of open space exacerbated by poor air quality left no healthy or sheltered places to play and develop emotional intelligence. This lacuna fostered the birth of Play-Live, which was later renamed Smaaash.

There were a few existing formats, but they lacked the neutrality of age and, most importantly, the application of modern available technology. Once, in 2011, while watching a cricket match, I saw the technology offered by Hawkeye and requested them to develop an expertise that would take indoor cricket to the next level.

At that time, Hawkeye was an independent company and they had the flexibility to move quickly. One-and-half-years of hard work followed which involved creating a special bowling simulator—that could bowl fast, swing, and spin; a ball that would not hurt and yet had the feel of a season ball, perfecting

---

* Larry G. Maguire, 'Dr Stuart Brown on The 7 Properties of Play', Human Performance, 7 February 2022, https://humanperformance. ie/the-properties-of-play/, accessed on 25 September 2025.

the tracking technology and placing the field using AI depending on the strength of one's shots as well as the opposing team's ability to do the field placement. The game was created at four levels to make it all-inclusive. Women, men, children, adults, grandparents, amateurs, beginners, and pros could all play and have fun together.

Fielders had four levels of intelligence. At a beginner level, he could drop a catch, but at an international level (pro level) his fielding would be compared to the best of fielders. Imagine Malinga bowling to your son at an amateur level, and he hits a stylish boundary that rolls past fielders, and then he looks at you for appreciation. The subsequent thumbs up and resounding ovation that he would get created a deep, unforgettable connection. That was the bond I was looking for.

And this is how the first game of Smaaash was born. I was so excited that I invited Sachin Tendulkar and his family to try the simulator.

Sachin Tendulkar had come to England for his final overseas tour and I invited him and his family to Winchester which is approximately 35 km from London.

Sachin saw his son play and said, 'this is 99 per cent as good as real.' Next, we had lunch at a four-star Michelin restaurant. It was especially kept open for lunch because the great Sachin Tendulkar was coming. Being vegetarian, I hated the food, but I was not there for the food. It was the collaboration with the cricket legend that I was interested in. This is how the partnership with the great Sachin Tendulkar was born in England and his then-agent helped formulate it at the earliest. I was in seventh heaven because the first two objectives of the company were achieved

— You get to play with cricket stars regardless of your calibre.

— The God of Cricket, but for me the God of EQ, had agreed
   to partner with the venture.

I took it as a good omen. God was smiling upon me once again.

In 2012–2013, Star TV was bidding aggressively for
BCCI cricket rights. Sony Entertainment, with whom I had
investment banking connections, had IPL rights back then.
These two channels seemed to be the best fit as partners to give
a holistic cricket experience to their viewers. They could watch
a match at Smaaash and then play with the stars of their choice.

I first sought a meeting with Sony and I was meeting the
CEO after a long time. He was not enthused by what we had to
offer, but I did not let that deter me. I sent an email to the CEO
of Star TV and had to wait four weeks to meet their COO
and the EA to the CEO. They were impressed with the way I
explained the technology and what I had to offer.

The Star team was keen to sample an experience, but
unfortunately, we did not have any nets installed in India. I
invited them to Winchester, where our prototype could be
experienced. They were scheduled to visit Amsterdam in ten days
for a trade fair of the International Broadcasting Association.

The CEO and COO were highly impressed with the
technology and requested me to set up the facility in Mumbai
around the time their global boss, J.M., short for James
Murdoch, was visiting Mumbai for a board meeting. They were
clear that the buy-in would be done by J.M.

I was game to take the risk—because risk-taking was the
only thing I knew. In a matter of two weeks, we not only set
up the cricket lane, but also a few other technologies that we
had perfected. This included our hologram technology where
we filmed a Bharatanatyam dancer.

The set was in Rajkamal Studio, Mumbai. That morning,
I had my heart in my mouth. This was a do-or-die moment

for me. I had never had a big brother—a financial or strategic advisor—and this would be my first business in which I would have a solid partner to back my endeavours.

J.M. greeted me with a cordial namaste. He was accompanied by the India business CEO and COO. I noticed that there were two BMWs for J.M. One was empty and followed the car in which J.M. was travelling in so that if his car got into mechanical trouble, he could switch cars immediately. J.M. and the Star team spent an hour-and-a-half at the set-up.

Then, J.M. and his team from Star India left for an internal board meeting that was to last till 6 p.m. I spent the entire day in anticipation. Time ticked away slowly and I was getting impatient. At 6 p.m., I called their COO. The moment I was asked to come to their office, I rushed in. A sponsorship deal of Rs 15 crore over five years for five centres was agreed upon. It was a whopping Rs 75-crore deal and gave me enough flexibility to introduce new technology and games. Moreover, I was told that they were so impressed by what we had developed that they saw us as potential technology partners for future projects.

Initially, Star was hands-on in the branding development process. The head of marketing thought that the name, 'Play Live' did not ring true and after much consideration, their agency came up with the name SMASH. However, the website address was unavailable and so we inserted another 'a'— SMAASH. Yet again, the website address was unavailable, so we tried 3As. The trinity of 'A' worked like magic and we had our website up and running. I even included the 3As in my presentation: Amazing, Awesome, Aspirational.

And this is how Play-Live was renamed and Smaaash was born.

Now was the time to find space. I wanted the first centre to be in South Mumbai. So at the set-up in Rajkamal Studios, I invited almost all potential landlords for their perusal. At that time, active entertainment was restricted to smaller areas and was mostly for toddlers and children. Moreover, landlords focused on passive entertainment like multiplex cinemas which were the flavour of the day. No landlord had an area of 20,000 square feet. It was now clear that the property of the first Smaaash would have to be outside a mall.

A broker took us to a property situated inside Kamala Mills. It was in shambles. KPMG had vacated the place a few years ago and it was a total mess. I knew that the fit-out cost would be extremely high, but the place had enormous advantages. It was in South Mumbai and had 20,000 square feet to offer. Of this, 11,000 square feet was open area out of which 5,000 square feet had FSI (Floor Space Index) attached to it which means I could do additional construction to that extent.

I just knew in my gut that Kamala Mills would be the home of my first Smaaash. That land was my *karmabhoomi* (place of action). However, it was an architectural challenge to fit more than four cricket lanes and so under the guidance of the first CEO (who worked in Dubai and then in India for an Indian conglomerate based in Dubai), we purchased a few arcade and redemption games.

Our USP was cricket but was that enough? I needed a few more stand-out attractions. After two months of global search, we got a Robokeeper—a robotic goalkeeper that was developed by a German University; an F-1 Racing Simulator that was developed by a French company; and finally, an Omni Directional Treadmill with a BB gun where one could play the popular game 'Call of Duty' with the BB gun having forced feedback. I referenced YouTube which helped me identify new games that were in the marketplace.

In November 2011, we had a party for select guests and members of the press. The CEO of Star as well as Sachin Tendulkar shared the dais with me for the opening on 12 November 2013. As I took a seat with the illustrious personality, the forty days of non-stop efforts humbled me. There were so many roadblocks we had to overcome while creating our first Smaaash centre. The greatest challenge was the infamous Mumbai rains and the subsequent deluge, which resulted in the centre being submerged in water. Thankfully, the team got water pumps and drained the water, saving the equipment from greater damage.

As we sat on the dais, Tendulkar spoke highly about the idea of Smaaash and how it was an honour and privilege for him to be associated with the brand. When the CEO was asked if Star would consider an equity investment, they diplomatically said that they would decide in times to come as anything was possible. My heart beat faster. Happiness coursed through my body—I had to make it happen. It was an evening I still remember with crystal clear clarity.

The next fifteen days were a disaster. No one knew where Kamla Mills was. Our ads were ineffective in their messaging as there was no footfall. My four guest relation officers and I would just stand at the entrance, introduce ourselves to passersby and offer to show them the facility. We got a handful of enthusiasts but by and large, the response was lukewarm. The food was outsourced to Sodexo. Their expertise lay in bulk corporate meals but they had zero experience in the running of a restaurant. We started on the wrong foot, as far as F&B was concerned.

A week later, the legendary political powerhouse of Maharashtra, Shri Balasaheb Thackeray passed away and the entire city came to a grinding halt during the mourning period.

I was used to business which generated hefty cash flow on a day-to-day basis. Now I was saddled with a centre no one knew—in terms of its location and what the hell it was all about. Some of our prospective clients thought we were a new channel launched by Star.

It was only after 25 November that the crowds started trickling in. My four guest relations executives and I were all set to show the space. The idea to offer a Harley Davidson bike ride to anyone who scored four goals against our Robokeeper and our cricket facilities ensured that we became the talk of the town. We came to be known as a male-centric place with cricket, soccer, and F1 racing becoming our key attractions. But there was nothing in it for ladies and the food was nothing to rave about.

Acting swiftly to appeal to non-cricket enthusiasts, we ordered six bowling lanes from Brunswick. We contacted their agent in India and said we needed to have the bowling lanes operational before 24 December. It was the 27 November already.

In a matter of ten days, the bowling alley was airlifted from Illinois (USA) and Szekesfehervar (Hungary). I did not look at the costs. I was determined that Smaaash would become a watering hole for everyone in the family. It had to have something in it for adults, children, and moms and dads to make it an age and gender-neutral avenue.

As there was no building, an entire tensile structure had to be erected. And so, in a matter of fifteen days, we not only built the structure but also air-conditioned it and got a bar license as well.

We were now ready for social gatherings in general and could cater to our female clientele as well. It was a revelation to us that people liked ten-pin bowling more than cricket. Secondly, the revenue from bowling was 2.5 times the revenue from cricket because in an area occupied by one cricket lane, we could fill two bowling lanes. Bowling gave a considerable push to our business.

News spread in the best way possible: word-of-mouth. Many notable landlords such as DLF, Inorbit, and G. Corp (Bangalore), offered us spaces. Unlike our Kamala Mills experience, where we had no say as we were novices, this time we flatly refused rentals and offered a fixed revenue share. Every mall agreed to the suggestion, but they asked for a common area maintenance fee, which was sometimes higher than the rent.

However, this time, we stuck to our stand and soon all the malls agreed to our revenue-sharing arrangement. Within six months, we opened centres in Hyderabad and Bangalore where we were given prime locations. There were several issues with DLF Noida mall, and though that was to come first after Mumbai, it took two years to materialize. We also opened a centre in Ludhiana.

After Mumbai, the next centre opened at Cybercity Gurgaon. At that time, my Parkinson's had spread to my legs, and my stability was weak. So I gave the job to the architects, a renowned project management company, and my team who were involved in the development of the Mumbai centre. I focused on staying in office, which was also my new research and development centre.

The foreign products were very expensive and cash was running out. The idea was to develop products locally instead of buying European ones and we hired two product consultants from the US and Sweden respectively. The entire R & D facility was headed by the former team of the now-defunct telecom venture.

The first blockbuster product was Finger Coaster, which was born along with three to four other products. The people in Gurgaon had more money and there would be more corporate and birthday parties at that location. Above all, CyberHub was not Kamla Mills; it already had an impressive footfall.

But just seven days before the commencement of operations, I went to CyberHub and realized that it was a complete mess!

The management of CyberHub appreciated my presence there standing with swollen feet, twenty-four hours a day to get the centre up and running. The PMC (project management company) and contractors had already taken us for a ride, but that was the least of my worries. I had to open centres in Bangalore and Hyderabad and I was getting persistent calls from Star to see them. My intuition told me that something was amiss.

I stayed till the inauguration of the CyberHub Centre. We had an impressive list of invitees and the reviews were fantastic. I flew from New Delhi to Hyderabad and then Bangalore to ensure that the crises did not repeat in those centres.

Finally, I met the Star TV guys. I knew that something was wrong because the COO did not see me, nor did the head of Star Sports. There was a cold welcome by the CMO, who, without beating around the bush, broke the news that Star wanted to terminate the contract as the new conscious decision within the organization was that the cost of the experiential marketing provided by Smaaash was astronomical as compared to other traditional means of marketing.

Besides Mumbai, they would not be sponsoring any more centres. I froze. I had payments to make and here the sponsorship deal was getting dropped. (This is the price one pays if one does not listen to the universal consciousness or god's consciousness). I said nothing. I left the meeting and dropped an email requesting a meeting with the CEO/COO. After much cajoling, I managed a meeting with the COO, which was attended by the CMO as well.

I showed them two photographs. A very young Sachin Tendulkar with a cricket bat and the second was the frenzy of young fans at a cricket game behaving like hooligans. I simply said, 'The call is yours. Do you want to build a nation of viewers or a nation of players? Ask your hearts and then answer me.' It was my trump card.

In due course, they agreed to do three centres for Rs 30 crore. The sponsorship numbers for the two incremental centres came down to Rs 7.5 crore each. I had no choice but to agree as I did not have the muscle to fight a multi-billion dollar media conglomerate. During this time, we also got an offer from a private equity fund based in Dubai which agreed to invest Rs 30 crore. Instead of repaying debt and reinstating the fund account, I opted to spend more on expansion.

Finally, the Noida centre opened but the mall had issues with a fire NOC, which was later resolved. We requested Sachin Tendulkar to inaugurate one of our upcoming centres. The God of Cricket pulled in the crowds and the place was bursting at the seams. There was no place to stand and people would do anything to get a selfie with him. We were in such a hurry to expand that in Bangalore, we overlooked the fact that the centre was not suitable for cricket and was spread over two floors.

Soon, problems started to crop up from all departments, be it revenue, talent, management, and cost escalations. After the initial excitement and euphoria, revenue started declining steadily. We roped in a consultant who was later made the CEO. His expertise was hotel management in general and F&B in particular, and thanks to him, our quality of food went up, and we aggressively marketed corporate and birthday parties. Our motto was 'RIP boring parties'. We would give the corporate guys an experience where a junior could defeat his boss and not be reprimanded. The corporate and birthday parties continue to remain a mainstay for Smaaash even today.

Experimenting with new games and experiences is very critical in our type of business, where revenue can dip on account of failure. I experimented with go-karting, paintball, laser tag, a children's area, and a snow park. However, none of them gave the desired impetus to revenue. Everyone knew of Smaaash. It was an aspirational brand, but the sentiment was not reflected in our revenue.

Except for Mumbai, all centres were on revenue share. So for rent, a certain percentage of revenue was fixed. However, Mumbai was bleeding at Rs 50–60 lakh per month at the earnings before interest, taxes, depreciation and amortization (EBIDITA) level. In short, the rent we were paying to the landlord was at a loss. So I struck a deal with the landlord and offered him 10 per cent equity. This would mean that Smaaash, inclusive of the Gujarati restaurant built in the shape of a train called Pravaas, 18.99 our conference centre, and our terrace restaurant Verbena, would also be rent-free for five years!

How did I finance all this? I raised approximately Rs 75 crore from a private equity investor and Rs 45 crore from a debt fund, which, in addition to creating a lien on the corporate assets, took a charge on all my homes. I also withdrew funds to the extent of Rs 20 crore and kept it aside for my wife and daughter in a trust account.

Thus, I created Smaaash, which was profitable at EBIDITA levels though the ROCE was extremely poor. That was due to the following reasons: space-guzzler games like cricket; and go-karting, SnowPark, Paintball and Laser Tag were not doing well on a revenue per square feet basis. Cricket would have given us revenue of Rs 300 per square foot while go-karting gave us Rs 95 per square foot. Food sales had increased, but it was not profitable. Amongst all the centres, Ludhiana was ignored the most and wore an outdated look from the 1990s.

Our capital expenditure (capex) was also very high. Leasehold improvisation expenses were approximately Rs 7,000–10,000 per square foot, which was humongous. I had scant experience with the project expense costs and had to rely solely on my team to work out if the costs were in sync. To add to this, there was a gaming capex of approximately Rs 7 crore per centre and R & D expenses of approximately Rs 60 lakh per month.

The high costs did not bother me. The brand experience needed to fly globally. I was a foolhardy, ambitious visionary in that sense, and thought that the expenses we had to incur were because of the advanced nature of the games. In tertiary discussions, everyone told me that Rs 7,000 to Rs 10,000 per square foot was the approximate leasehold improvement cost.

Instead of looking to reduce costs at capex and other levels—I was looking to expand overseas where my private equity fund based in Dubai was well acquainted with the Emaar Group. The Emaar Group was creating four theme parks, including a Bollywood park for Expo 2020. They even floated a billion-dollars-worth IPO on the Dubai Stock Exchange.

They favourably considered our proposal to set up a Smaaash centre, which by then had become a leader in sports games and VR games in the prime location of Sheikh Zayed Road. They were even willing to offer substantial capex support. This was a godsend and in 2015 we signed the deal on Eid!

From then on, I made over twenty-five trips to Dubai, for some reason or the other. Either it was a change in management, locations, or terms of agreement. All this time god/the universe was sending signals, as if asking me *'What the f**k are you doing? Don't you know you're on the path to ruin?'*

But I ignored the signs. I was driven by emotion, not logic, and what I thought was intuition, was in reality a gamble.

Not focusing on our Indian centres resulted in a month-on-month decline in revenues. Mumbai was beginning to look like a wreck and the other centres also needed a refreshment of content. Ludhiana never took off, and there was pilferage in our Delhi centres (which we discovered later during Covid-19). The mall owners, such as DLF and Inorbit, were also complaining about a decline in revenue. I did not pay much attention and driven by ego, I went to the US to establish a Smaaash centre, which would be a million-dollar-a-month revenue generator, or so I thought.

In New Jersey, I happened to meet an interesting family of Iranian Jews who had migrated to the US immediately after the fall of the Shah of Iran. There were 108 members of the Ghermezian family. All of them worked under one roof in East Rutherford, New Jersey. They were developing a mall in New Jersey and they owned the Mall of America (Minneapolis) and Edmonton Mall (Canada). I met the senior most family member who oversaw leasing. He had a magnetic personality and like a tantrik he would succeed in getting me under his spell. I was enamoured by this sixty-year-old gentleman. So desperate was I to start the global presence of Smaaash that I overlooked due diligence. This was the costliest mistake that I would make in my entire life. Here was a landlord risen from the depths of despair, whose family was involved in many charities, and above all, they were so god-fearing—how could I not trust them? Little did I realize that they were extremely shrewd businessmen who had cut their teeth on Iranian soil.

Around that time, our prime minister, Narendra Modi, announced demonetization. Our business came to a grinding halt in India and my conviction to open the centre in the US strengthened.

The space offered to me in Mall of America would normally be offered at no more than $40,000 rental. I was offered it at four times that value and I took it without negotiating. There were going to be lease improvement charges as well which ordinarily malls in the US were accustomed to bearing then and even now.

Unfortunately, I got none. This is what happens when you let emotions take over your mind and overpower your intellect and rationale.

In -40-degree Celsius weather, my team and I toiled day in and day out from 5 a.m. to midnight to ensure we met the December timeline. It was the toughest construction I have seen in my life. One time, we had to open the roof of the mall, so that the heavy steel material to build the go-karting track could be let in. It was done post-midnight and completed by 7 a.m. My team was working hard, and I was present every step of the way to ensure that their morale was high. The governor of Minneapolis was so impressed with our technology that he announced 14 November 2016 as 'Shripal Morakhia Day'. However, the project was doomed from the word 'go'. From an estimate of Rs 40 crore, the project cost shot up to Rs 108 crore! This meant that unless we did a million dollars a month, we would not break even. All revenue forecasts given by a professional agency fell flat and we managed to achieve no more than 20 per cent of the revenue.

Within four months from the date of possession, we were ready to open the centre in Minneapolis, in late December. On 22 December 2016, we opened our doors to the USA's first 'double-decker go-karting track'. It occupied three-fourths of the area, while VR and sports games took the balance. Despite paying skyrocketing rentals, we were not allowed the luxury of having arcade games.

Back then, Minneapolis had high employment of 98 per cent and most of the ground staff we were forced to hire had a criminal record. To make matters worse, it was illegal to ask a potential employee if they had a criminal record. The staff was highly irresponsible and the quality of managers we attracted— well, the less said the better.

Our machines were labour intensive, and at any given time, we needed twenty-five operators. Forget the numbers, the quality of staff we attracted was pathetic.

The go-karting track was designed for skill. In the US, they love pushing the pedal and accelerating the kart. However, ours was a narrow track that did not allow that luxury, as it was designed by an European expert.

We were very thin on management, not just in India but in the US as well. Our CEO resigned because he was diagnosed with oral cancer. The second CEO, who was a scion of a hotel empire, joined us just to spite his father, and negotiate a deal with him. He was media-hungry and his only obsession was to make sure he was written about in the press. The second obsession was food tasting (as we were opening the Gujarati restaurant). When the pressure started to mount, within six months of the US launch, he quit.

To top it all, my second-in-command of operations was involved in a sex scandal with a female employee and we had no other option but to fire him.

I was so naïve and driven that only after we opened, did I realize that the place rented to us had been abandoned for sixteen years. I could have leased it for a pittance.

The US was a huge mistake. A blunder of unimaginable proportions had been made by me that single-handedly led to the downfall of Smaaash in the years to come. I had increased my borrowings from another set of debt funds to Rs 125 crore at the Smaaash level and Rs 25 crore at the holding company level. My monthly interest liability alone was Rs 1.5 crore and I needed $15 million of revenue from US operations to simply be able to breathe easily.

Within three months of opening the US centre, my team and I agreed that it was a disaster. We had to hide this from the world. But if anyone thought that was the solution—well, it proved to be fatally wrong.

My downfall had only just begun.

13

Fire in Mumbai and the Subsequent Revival of Smaaash

In each moment the fire rages, it will burn away a hundred veils.
And carry you a thousand steps towards your goal.

—Rumi

2017–2018

By February 2017, Smaaash was sinking bit by bit. After the US operations, debt had spiralled to Rs 185 crores! I was doling out Rs 2 crore as monthly interest payments and Rs 90 lakh in rent per month for the US operations. We had appointed Indian investment bankers who were looking to float an IPO. However, they had reasonable doubts and questions to which I had no answers. The Ludhiana centre was a non-starter and all the other centres looked dilapidated. I distinctly remember when the father of one of the boys at a birthday party at Smaaash commented that the party room in Mumbai looked like the BEST canteen. The other centres were also a mess and the content was not refreshed. We were looking not only jaded but unkempt as well, despite minor refreshes here and there.

The go-karting track needed urgent refurbishment. It had potholes that we would temporarily fill up. Our maintenance cost of go-karting was a whopping 16 per cent of the monthly P&L account.

Instead of investing aggressively in India, our focus was more on upgrading the MOA centre in the US to make it profitable. We introduced ten other games and a conventional laser tag arena in the hope that we would at least reach half a million dollars in revenue. We were clocking $1,50,000–$2,00,000 of turnover per month after a stellar opening. In summer and even in the fall, everyone wanted to be outdoors. The footfall of the mall fell considerably and our revenues were southward of $1,00,000.

By then, I could sense impending doom. Nothing was going right. My poised appearance belied the havoc in my mind and I was a nervous wreck.

However, we were extremely good at financial engineering—our profits always showed increments because whatever expenses we could capitalize on as per the law, we did. Our P&L account looked very healthy, but the balance sheet was beginning to bloat. For that year, we showed an EBIDTA (earnings before interest, depreciation and taxes) of Rs 10 crore by capitalizing expenses to the extent of Rs 35 crore. This included a sponsorship of Rs 30 crore and profit from the sale of equipment to cruise companies to the extent of Rs 2 crore. Financially, we were unsound and it reflected in our bulging balance sheet. I had to do further financial engineering to save my skin.

It was then that we got an offer to buy eight bowling alley locations that belonged to a joint venture between a Thai-based bowling company and the largest multiplex chain in India.

Simultaneously, my CFO got an offer to buy six south-based centres located in Telangana and Karnataka. I lapped up the opportunity—stock markets and liquidity were at a peak and I was confident that somehow, I would be able to raise liquidity. The asking price for both properties was Rs 110 crore. I was getting 15 centres for the prices at which a 40,000 square feet facility was set up in Mall of America, Minneapolis.

Without knowing how I was going to raise the resources, I decided to take the plunge. It was at this time that I hired a CEO who was in the multiplex chain referred to earlier. Before that, he was working for another multiplex chain which is now defunct. I had met him ten years ago as an investment banker when I was raising funds for that multiplex company. I hired him blindly and we started working on the acquisitions and raising finances for it. It was apparent that the bowling alley was not making money without the sponsorship income from a known beverage brand. Unlike our financial model, its rents were fixed and had huge common maintenance area charges. Rent was approximately 35 per cent of the revenues as compared to the US where it was 12–13 per cent of the revenues. Our centre in Cyberhub Gurgaon overlapped with their Gurugram centre. In a small city like Ludhiana, we would end up having two centres. I knew I was overpaying, but to hide our mistake, I had to plunge into this deal which would hopefully show us in a good light. The southern centre had one premium property and the rest were sub-standard. But that single property was making more money than our Mumbai centre.

It is with this southern centre's acquisition that I got someone who knew what makes a family entertainment complex click. Someone whose advice I relied on till my last day at work. As soon as the whiff of the deal leaked into the market, I was flooded with inquiries for debt. That was the peak time for NBFC funding. All NBFCs were getting phenomenal liquidity from banks and the public by accessing the debt and equity marketplace.

One debt fund belonging to a holistic financial services company which had not raised the funds till that time was in the race to find us. Finally, we selected a financial services company whose promoter was known to me. I was treated like a king in his office and it was as if they were desperate to lend to me. They had their resources tied up and were willing to move very fast—in short, they were willing to match my speed.

Against the same assets—my four flats and the Lonavala property—they agreed to give Rs 220 crore to Smaaash and Rs 50 crore to my holding company. Things were moving at such breakneck speed that I did not even forward them a copy of the legal and commercial due diligence. This was an extremely large deal and their team was motivated to seal the deal. There was some problem with the quality of one of the additional collaterals that we were to offer, nevertheless, they agreed to go ahead and disburse the money. The brokerage firm referred to earlier whose debt fund had not closed decided to participate in our growth story by raising equity for us at a Rs 700 crore equity valuation. The stock markets were bullish and investors wanted more and more paper and were willing to invest in private companies also. We mutually agreed to a valuation of Rs 700 crore equity based on the future projection of the company. I must have met approximately 100 investors in Mumbai, Ahmedabad and Kolkata of which 20 per cent felt it was expensive and 8 per cent read the due diligence report and realized our modus operandi of capitalizing on costs. Despite the balance sheet and the P&L account not being in great shape we were able to raise Rs 200 crore. The world thought that we had become a prosperous company. The earlier two lenders asked for a Rs 7.5 crore pre-payment charge. In September 2016, we were the proud owners of twenty centres—nineteen in India and one in the USA. The perception we succeeded in creating was that we were an Indian brand destined to succeed anywhere, be it in an advanced country, the financial capital of India, or its smaller cities. There was a certain excitement about Smaaash.

YES Bank came forward and increased their exposure from Rs 15 crore to Rs 45 crore. That very month, YES Bank introduced me to SPAC—a blank cheque company that had raised Rs 50 million from a bunch of US investors and was also listed on NASDAQ. Whilst the promoters of a blank cheque company could propose investments to buy corporates wholly or partially, investors had the option to redeem their holdings. The catch was that while the fund was in the bank, if the investors did not like the investee company, they could pull out and the sponsors would have to find new investors. The sponsors were two Indians—Jacob Cherian and Suhel Kanuja. They showed fancy office addresses on their visiting cards. Jacob was adept at name-dropping and gave the impression that he knew everyone who mattered in financial circles. He would provide instances as to how he could do the impossible and I was impressed with him at the first meeting. I travelled to NYC to meet the lead underwriter, Maxim, who assured me that the issue would do well. Moreover, he insisted that no SPAC issue had failed and India was beginning to get hot. During my first trip, I realized that Jacob Cherian was a house-husband whose primary occupation was to look after his three daughters, as his wife was an extremely successful medical practitioner. The office address was the address of their lawyer and our meetings were conducted at Starbucks. Back in September 2017, when I returned, my instincts told me that what I was getting into was not good for me. I started looking for other options. After all, the India IPO would be difficult as the ROE and ROCE were poor and there was no same-store growth. We also had to prove our management skills in handling the enhanced scope of operations.

The SPAC guys were bowled over by what the company had to offer. In the meantime, the bankers who got us the debt were keen on us meeting a group of strategic Chinese Investors who had, amongst other investments, several successful malls in their portfolio. I went with my team and made a presentation. We saw several properties in China, and by the time we came back, the Indo-Chinese relationship went for a toss, and their investment in a pharma company in India was also not getting clearance. The deal fell through at a nascent stage, and I was left with no other option but to take resources from SPAC, though I had very little faith in their promoters.

During this time, my chief technology officer (CTO) and chief financial officer (CFO) found certain immoral actions associated with our CEO. I was left with no other option but to fire him. By now I was completely out of the day-to-day running of the company and the entire task of integrating the two acquisitions was left in the hands of my CFO and CTO. I was occupied with SPAC and the formalities associated with them and so, 2018 and 2019 were hectic years.

In December 2017, after three years of relentless hard work, I decided to take a break with my entire family: wife, daughter, son-in-law and two granddaughters. I hoped the Scandinavian trip would usher in a new chapter in my life. We reached on 25 December, Christmas morning. It was 29 December in the small Finnish town of Unnisaari when we took a dip in freezing waters and followed up that with a sauna.

Just as I was warming myself with a sip of Finnish-style vegetarian soup, my mobile phone rang. I disconnected it as I was on a much-deserved holiday. It was only after the caller on the other end relentlessly called non-stop that I answered. Someone was desperately trying to reach me from the office.

I was shocked at what the caller said and my heart sank. A massive fire had engulfed a portion of Kamla Mills and many lives had been lost.

Luckily, the fire was nowhere close to our centre and we thought we would not be affected. I discussed it with my team and concluded that there was nothing to worry about as our papers were impeccable. However, that night at 3 a.m., sleep eluded me. There was a nagging feeling that all was not well. Moments later, I got a call from the office again. Fifteen people had died in the Kamla Mills fire, and there were strict instructions to punish the guilty. Our statutory authorities are known to take knee-jerk responses, and I voiced my fear to the team. We had a special officer to liaise with statutory authorities for Kamla Mills. At 6:30 a.m. CET, I got a call that they had started demolishing our outer area. The demolition of the Gujarati restaurant, Pravaas was inevitable. A message had to be sent out that the Sachin-Tendulkar-backed-Smaaash (that is how we were still known to the press) had also not been spared by the BMC. I woke my wife up and said I had to leave. She agreed that I had no choice as she scrolled through the damage in the photographs sent to me on WhatsApp.

From my picturesque Finnish town sojourn, it was a four-hour drive to Helsinki. From Helsinki, I flew to London. There, I had to wait for another six hours at Heathrow, before boarding a flight to Delhi. From Delhi, a three-hour wait before I boarded yet another plane for Mumbai. When I finally arrived, I had been travelling for thirty-six hours non-stop.

The next morning, I was at the Kamla Mills Smaaash at 8.30 a.m. Without exaggeration, the scene was reminiscent of the carnage caused by a serial bomb blast. Pravaas was demolished beyond recognition and the trampoline park was destroyed. I kept my cool in front of my team. Inside, I was a broken man. When my wife called me around noon, I could not hold back my tears. I kept asking *why me?* She asked me to be strong and move ahead towards the restoration of Smaaash.

One of the owners of Kamla Mills had been jailed and the other, with four of his nephews, had gone underground. How was I to move ahead? My liaison officer and I went to the BMC office. They were also threatening to demolish the conference facility and the terrace restaurant and I quickly got a stay order from the Bombay High Court.

Everyone felt that the BMC had acted with undue haste. The law provided for a three-week notice period to rectify errors committed by the landlord or the tenant.

I wrote a handwritten letter to the BMC commissioner, and he asked me to see his deputy, who orally authorized and informed my ward office to allow us rehabilitation work. We started it in full swing, and in twelve days, Smaaash was rebuilt! Furthermore, it had never looked swankier. We put up a big photo of the fire department approval to put people's fears to rest.

Several parties and events were cancelled. The start was slow, but our PR on social media was very effective. By 15 January 2018, within less than ten days of operation, we were back in action. I kept every shareholder in the loop, and at that time, everyone was extremely supportive. But it took a huge toll financially, as we had to spend Rs 6 crore on the revival of the centre.

After reopening I was convinced that I had started attracting Murphy's law (anything that can go wrong, will go wrong.)

— the low value at which I sold my financial services business
— my telecom investment
— my movie production unit which I had shut
— ACK where I was in dispute with the partner
— the blow I received in the reduced value of my digital company
— the demonetization that distracted

— the way the MOA team took advantage of my naivete
— the real identity of my SPAC sponsors that I found whilst
  in NYC
— the fire in Mumbai and surprisingly why Smaaash was
  affected by it.

I could not fathom what was happening to me. The only optimistic people around me were my panel of astrologers who felt that nothing would go wrong in my life and I blindly believed them. I had no option, after all, it is only hope that helps us cope when life falls apart.

14

Smaaash Post-Fire

Black and white are the colours of photography. To me they symbolize the alternatives of hope and despair to which mankind is forever subjected.

—Robert Frank

January 2018–December 2018

Smaaash Mumbai was operating in full swing, generating revenues equal to the pre-mishap period. My shareholders, old and new, were appeased and so were the lenders. However, the cash reserves of the company were quickly depleting because of the renovations of the newly acquired centres, coupled with the legal and financial due diligence of the proposed merger with SPAC. This due diligence was as per US law, but it came at a hefty price of approximately Rs 12 crore.

Unfortunately, despite the renovation of 50 per cent of the area in each of the newly acquired centres, where we had removed 50 per cent of the bowling lanes and added Smaaash-specific products like cricket lanes, VR arcades, laser tag, and many more, the results were negligible on incremental revenues.

The other tragedy to hit us was that post the fire, our two cash cows in Mumbai—the conference centre, Verbana, the hookah bar, and Pravaas had been shut down as the BMC refused to renew the temporary license of the place. I believe that the landlord was understandably scared after the fire. Kamla Mills was split into two parts: the part where our facilities were located up to the passport office—went to one brother and his four nephews. The other brother took up another giant slice of the property. The infamous fire had divided this parcel of land.

Before going to the US for our proposed NASDAQ offering, I took one more chance with the local market. I met the 'Big Bull' and a fund that had invested in the pre-IPO offering of a virtual gaming company was finally hitting the market after seven years of delay.

The fund office was in the same compound as Smaaash. During my pitch presentation, the fund manager played a game on his mobile. His body language was such that even before I began, I knew he was not interested.

After a gap of nearly thirty years, I called up the 'Big Bull' and went to meet him with my CFO at his Nariman Point office. I remember him as a charming young man pulsating with life-force energy. Seated in his office now, he was a pale shadow of his former self. The 'Big Bull' was barely able to walk and needed an assistant for support. His lips and teeth were stained brown and red with paan masala. A crumpled shirt clung to his body.

We reminisced about the 1980s when I had returned from the USA. Back then, we would occasionally bump into each other below the stock exchange building. With utmost conviction, he spelled out why Tata Power was an excellent buy. In those days, it had been regarded as a widow's stock that was purchased for dividends, and for many years, it traded below par. He remembered those days with nostalgia. A few minutes into the conversation, we were joined by the CEO of his firm. The 'Big Bull' instructed the CEO to conduct a detailed research on our centres and only thereafter would he take a call whether to invest in our IPO. A three-member team was deployed for the due diligence.

I had hoped against hope that the investment would be made based on my pitch and not detailed due diligence. I knew that the three experienced analysts working with the 'Big Bull', who had made so many multi-bagger investments earlier, would not rate Smaaash as investment-worthy. A company that had raised approximately Rs 560 crore had a return on capital employed of less than 6 per cent at the EBIDITA level. They also detected unproductive assets that required accelerated depreciation, and until we were EBIDITA positive, profit at net level was a distant dream.

I knew that their answer would be a resounding no and yet, when I heard it, I was heartbroken. The only option was the USA, and at least Jacob and Suhel were extremely optimistic about the issue. With no options, I allowed myself to be infected with their enthusiasm.

I was taken to NASDAQ and photographed with its CEO and my name was splashed on the big screen. My CFO and I were now brimming with confidence.

Jacob and Suhel claimed that they took me to NASDAQ as they and Maxim had spoken to several investors and were confident of fixing the issues. I fixed up a meeting with a fund manager whom I had known since my SSKI days in Seattle. Maxim set up another meeting with the founder of an online travel booking company. I distinctly remember that the meeting in Seattle was on the 9 July. On 8 July, my birthday,

I prayed fervently for my luck to change—my astrologers had also predicted the beginning of a good time.

Jacob and his family invited me for lunch where Suhel was also present. Jacob's wife was the breadwinner. He had worked a decade-and-a-half-ago with a leading US firm, and even during lunch, he dropped a handful of big names that he would contact. It was a waste of time. All I did was make small talk with Jacob's wife and his three daughters.

Post lunch, I took a flight to Seattle and was fully prepped for my meeting on 11 July 2018 at 9 a.m. sharp. The meeting went on for a day-and-a-half. The fund manager told me in no uncertain terms that this was the wrong vehicle for listing. Of late, the bulk of SPAC issues were trading below par.

Though I am known as a financial wizard, it was in this meeting that I understood the SPAC structure. And once I could fit the pieces of the jigsaw, I knew that I was doomed. The promoters of SPAC had free shares and warrants amounting to 100 per cent of the company. The subscribers could redeem their shares before the merger. The free shares along with a warrant attached to the initial investment could be encashed by them post-merger. Thus, the fully diluted value for the SPAC holders would be a whooping Rs 1,200 crore after adjusting freebies.

That was the day I was convinced that Murphy's Law was in full force and everything that had to go wrong would. The next two months went in a series of meetings with lawyers, the sales team, and selling the issue. We included Maxim, ICICI, and one more Philadelphia-based investment banking firm, Montgomery Scott. To meet investors, I travelled between NYC, Boston, San Francisco, Texas, Los Angeles, and eight other cities in the USA, and two more in Canada. Wherever we found hope, we dashed there to give a pitch presentation. This was when I realized that Jacob and Suhel knew nothing; they were relying on Maxim, who did not know the Indian market. The only silver lining was that after my presentation, I was applauded for the technology and the steadfast resolve to make Smaaash into a global brand.

One Indian fund manager of a leading fund told me how I was chasing a mirage. Jacob had floated a SPAC before and had invested in an Indian stockbroking firm but had been removed from the board as he had made a mess of the SPAC. The news hit me like a bolt from the blue.

I got YES Bank on the phone and we spoke to Jacob and Suhel who assured us that the past would not haunt us anymore and that the issue would close shortly. They added that we should be focused on the issue and not on rumours surrounding the two promoters. After spending so much time and money, I had no option but to believe them.

As I was in the taxi going back to the hotel, I realized that before Smaaash, I had relied on intuition for all my other ventures. I do not know when I began relying on emotions and ego. That night, my blood pressure shot up to 150/100. Upset, Kalpana flew out to be with me and accompanied me to my meeting with Suhel, who flaunted his bank balance of $49 million and insisted that the issue would be subscribed. Strangely, Jacob refused to come on the line.

On the advice of Maxim and to make the issuance more palatable, we carried two more amendments in the documents filed with the SEC. The issue was then stretched by two to three months. All this came at an astronomical cost. We were scraping the bottom of the barrel. We had promised sixty centres by March 2019 and signed aggressively for centres in India to meet our commitment to potential investors. In the meantime, we completed our meeting with all potential investors and the sales team of the US-based broking house. ICICI had a one-member team who would accompany me to all the meetings. These bankers would spend time and money on breakfast and lunch meetings instead of creating a strategy for sales. No figures were coming to me as to the extent of subscription.

The issue, which was supposed to close in August, showed no sign of progress even in October. Surprisingly, by the end of September, our enthusiasm reached a new peak. From being buried in pessimism, suddenly, I had a lot of hope. An Indian fund manager based out of Boston visited our Mumbai centre and loved our technology of cricket, soccer, and VR. He wanted to meet—his fund was one of the first investors in Google.

The next day, I flew in with the two promoters of SPAC and gave my presentation. I was constantly interrupted by Jacob, who would interject and say, 'Shripal is a humble man . . . he is a big man. There is a Wikipedia page on him.' Big deal! Who was interested in trivia regarding me? Everyone wanted to know about the company and its way forward.

I was very honest and told him that I had learned while I had earned—the ROCE was low, but with our learnings it would shoot up. He believed in me. It was the best meeting I had so far where someone was forthcoming.

After my extraordinary meeting in Boston, I flew back to NYC. I was resting in my hotel room when the phone started to ring incessantly. My office was trying to reach me. ILFS, a non-banking financial company, a semi-statutory organization, and the largest in India, had defaulted. The stock markets had taken a huge hit, and the rupee was falling. In fact, in the next ten days, there was a sea change in the marketplace. Small caps, mid-caps and the market, in general, had collapsed. Our valuation had fallen by the wayside, and the rupee was in free fall. Whatever hopes I had after the Boston meeting were crushed. I knew at that very moment that I was doomed. It was October 2018. On 28 February 2019, Rs 110 crore of my debt would fall due.

I stayed back in NYC and tried other ways to raise resources. Many malls in the USA had large spaces available and were willing to give us an incentive to invest in them. I must have screened seven to eight properties, but I could not focus. I was down to earning and paying, the company had no bank balance to speak of. We were defaulting on rent and I was constantly on calls with the landlords, giving them a rosy picture of what was going on and assuring them that the rent would be paid shortly. Our monthly salaries were Rs 4.5 crore; rent was another Rs 6 crore and utilities amounted to Rs 1.5 crore. When you do not pay rent, the mall disconnects your power during operating hours. So in the middle of the night (for me, since I was in the US), I had to speak to the mall management team to give me a few days. MOA owners were also threatening us with termination as nearly $5,00,000 was owed to them.

While this was going on, the two promoters of SPAC wanted my cooperation to close the issue. They wanted me to consider a merger with an e-sports gaming company.

I met them in Florida and realized it was a start-up that had barely invested one-quarter of a million dollars in the venture. Their CEO was like a typical used-car salesman, and the promoter looked like a nefarious character straight from *The Godfather*.

It was perhaps late October or early November. I had had enough and put my foot down. There were a few more meetings and presentations lined up and I cancelled them, and two days later, I was on a flight to Mumbai. There was a sense of déjà vu. I had the same feeling in the pit in my stomach when I was flying to Mumbai after the news of my father's demise. I was staring into pitch darkness without a sliver of light.

Everything had gone wrong after the acquisition. There was no sizeable improvement in revenue. There were defaults left, right and centre, including statutory defaults. The older centres needed a massive facelift. There was no money left, and major debt repayment was coming up in less than three months. To exacerbate the issue, the operating team at the non-banking financial company that had lent me capital had changed. The new guy's only job was to pester me and I would get calls at all times in NYC. Once I was in back in Mumbai, all hell broke loose.

At the age of sixty-two, when I planned to bask in the glory of retirement, I was gaping into a deep abyss. Seven months of effort was reduced to dust. By listening to my emotions, I had merely postponed the problem. I did not know how I was going to resolve the impending problem of Rs 110–140 crore overdue loan apart from the Rs 30 crore I needed for operations.

It was a self-goal. All the time, the universe had been subtly sending messages, but I had ignored them. When bad times come, you think of it as a blip. The good times are a blip actually, and the bad ones linger on endlessly.

From the new heights of India's first global Family Entertainment Centre (FEC) brand with Sachin Tendulkar as a brand ambassador, a private equity fund on board, a queue to lend or invest in the company, two acquisitions simultaneously—I was now on the brink of a fall and it looked like there would be no return.

15

Smaaash after the Nasdaq Debacle

Many flared problems, but found more despair:

Don't run from snakes straight to a dragon's lair!

—Rumi

December 2018–April 2020

This was the second time in my life when I had come back to Mumbai from NYC with broken wings, but unlike the last time, now I had my family. I looked forward to meeting my wife and daughter and my two beautiful granddaughters. Ironically, just as with my daughter, I had missed watching them grow.

The high point of the US trip was that Smaaash's name, as well as mine, flashed in high definition on the display wall of NASDAQ right in the middle of Times Square! After the advertisement, Jacob had a meeting with the president of NASDAQ where the 'bell' ceremony of our listing was discussed. He asked me to request Sachin Tendulkar to ring the bell. This was the peak of my stay in NYC.

At the same time, all investors of SPAC had redeemed their stock. The true identity of the promoters of SPAC was revealed and this was when Jacob went entirely berserk. I had taken the failure in my stride, but Jacob was unable to do so and blamed the high debt of the company for the failure of the issue. He was constantly accusing me of doing a side deal with his co-promoters.

One day at our 'office', Jacob was livid. With no money in the bank, they went ahead with the listing based on the free shares. They merged with a start-up gaming company and the market capitalization on OTC listing (the company even cancelled the NASDAQ listing) for less than a hundred thousand dollars.

Given this ugliness—in four months I not only put on 10 kilos, but started suffering from high blood pressure as well. Now back in Mumbai, I landed within the solace of my wife's company, the only balm in my life. Once the news of a failed issue leaked into the market, malls began haunting me for a payment schedule for the unpaid rentals. Failing that, they warned, they would evict us. A Malayali gentleman from Kerala who was hired by one of the NBFCs from whom I had availed of the loan was constantly calling about the status of the Rs 10 crore payment.

The next day, I requested an ex-employee in SSKI to loan me Rs 20 crore to sort out the mess. He agreed to loan me Rs 5 crore and an additional Rs 7 crore came from the main investor. With this, I was able to pay salaries and 50 per cent of the dues to all the malls. My residual assets aggregated to Rs 5 crore and my wife's family supported me with Rs 9 crore. I had just enough to move things along for a quarter. The business was weighed down by salaries and rents—especially the US rentals—as a percentage of the revenue that it appeared like an impossible task to revive it. To exacerbate the situation, I was physically and mentally exhausted.

Politics had seeped into the office and my CTO was responsible—whom I had regarded as a son and CEO designate. He had free access to everyone, including the investors, and he bad-mouthed me, telling everyone how I had screwed over the fortunes of the company. Office politics had reached such a horrendous level that sometimes I did not feel as if I was in my own office.

In the meantime, meetings with the NBFC became difficult to handle. In one of their meetings, their chief legal officer put his legs on the table, his shoes facing me, and said that the time had come to transfer all my properties to the NBFC's name. I politely told him that we would do whatever was right. In another meeting, one of the top brass of the NBFC called me a *'chor'* (thief) and started interrogating me and my CFO, using extremely foul language. I got up and just walked out of the meeting, telling him, 'this is no way to deal with a man of integrity who is fifteen years your senior.' Once the due date for principal repayment had passed, the mental harassment increased manifold.

It was at this time, that the founder of the 'holistic' brokerage firm that had raised Rs 200 crore of equity, met with investors/directors. They insisted that the company needed a CEO and so an expensive head-hunting firm was hired to do so.

My inner voice reasoned that in the absence of resources, what would the CEO do? More importantly, the company had just cut the salaries of existing employees to make them more affordable. In this situation, how could we afford a high-flying CEO? They all wanted a capital market-friendly CEO, especially from an online firm which was the flavour of the markets those days.

The first person I was supposed to meet in Delhi was the head of a fashion division of the company that had been acquired by the US giant Walmart. He was no longer a part of the company after the restructuring. I wasted time, money and energy because when I went to Delhi, I was told that he was unwell and the meeting had to be cancelled. There was no talk of postponing or rescheduling.

I then met other candidates; two from Bangalore. One of them was an interesting person who claimed he had taken his foreign brand way ahead of the two large competing sportswear companies. Globally, the company he represented was the smallest of the three, but back home, he had ensured that it became the largest among the three. He was avaricious and set forth many preconditions. He wanted a salary of Rs 5 crore, which was Rs 50 lakh higher than the current salaries of all my employees combined.

Then, he wanted the office to be shifted to Bangalore, with a COO and CMO of his choice; all investments in the subsidiary that would conduct the digital business; 75 per cent of the holdings to be in his nominees' names subject to a ceiling of Rs 50 crore and if that was not enough, an obscene amount of ESOPs in Smaaash. He claimed that his knowledge of marketing and operations would convert Smaaash into a powerhouse recreation centre. I truly wanted to believe him. And I truly wanted to give my responsibilities to someone else—but was this cost something my company could even afford at that moment?

I thought my advisors would turn him down. Instead, they agreed to pursue his candidature and after a one-on-one meeting, they unanimously thought that Smaaash should hire him. I kept asking if Smaaash could afford such a high-flier. Just to be able to afford him and the team, he would have to increase our revenues by 200 per cent.

How was this going to be feasible? And in case he wanted the centres to be refurbished to achieve this objective—how were we going to fund the capex at a time even when day-today operations were difficult to fund? I knew where we had gone wrong and knew how to rectify it, but I had lost the courage to stand up.

However, my investors were pleased with his credentials and asked me to pursue him. On his part, he coaxed the seven of us to come to Bangalore, instead of him alone coming to Mumbai. Under pressure from my investors, my team and I went to explain to him the dynamics of the business. We presented to him all the reasons for our failure and the inability to capture the first movers' advantage. He smiled and stated, 'That is your weakness. That is why I am being hired to replace you.' I kept my mouth shut. That day I made up my mind that I would not hire him, regardless of the hardships I would have to endure. I needed a team-builder and not a smug individual who came with the impression that he was god's gift to Smaaash.

Next, the investors and their nominee's interference in the business were creating a massive division in the organization. Unanimously, the belief was that I was single-handedly responsible for the state of the company.

This made the 'holistic' broking firm owner demand that I transfer my entire holdings to his clients, so that they would hold approximately 58 per cent of the company as opposed to their current holding of 20 per cent.

Little did they realize that all entertainment companies went through this phase. Dave and Busters, the biggest entertainment company in the US also took a similar path of growth through debt, while Six Flags, another entertainment company, also had a string of bankruptcies before it became a stable stock market darling.

Smaaash had committed a huge blunder—a blunder of unimaginable proportions by investing a sum of Rs 108 crore in the US—50 per cent more than its original planned investment. I realized that unless something was done to mitigate the losses it would be difficult to survive. After a heated argument with the owners of Mall of America, they reduced the rentals but not retrospectively.

Our maximum revenues in winters averaged to $2,00,000 and in summers to $70,000 dollars. I told the owners of Mall of America, that for us to survive, the rent would have to be down to $30,000 dollars and that too with retrospective effect. This was the rent our next-door bowling and arcade company was paying and owing to my stupidity of relying on the owners, I was making a much higher payment. I even threatened that in case this was not done, I would be forced to shut shop.

They did not relent. We were thin on managerial and financial resources and the losses needed to be cut drastically. Therefore, I decided to close the US operation. What was to have been a game changer had turned into the cause of my doom. It was a loss of face, capex and apex investments. And above all, it was a personal loss for me. I had trusted the Ghermezians and I had taken them at face value.

I admit that I had let my investors, lenders and employees down. Above all, I had fallen in my own eyes. It became difficult to get out of bed in the mornings, but I was tenacious and stuck to my ground. The cruise ship contracts gave us much-needed profits and that year, we completed a $4 million shipment to Saudi Arabia. The richest man in India purchased bowling lanes and bumper cars from us. All this gave us much-needed funds to pay our expenses as the revenue from operations was being invested in capex that we had committed at the time of the NASDAQ issue. I should have stopped the unwarranted capex, but when you are depressed and anxious, no decision is ever right—especially when the people to whom you have given responsibility have ulterior motives.

I had truly lost hope for Smaaash in America. I learned that the mall owners were giving incentives to open shops within their premises. I wanted to set up an indoor water park with an automated sliding roof, so that it became outdoors in the summer. I had a vision of Smaaash building 1,00,000 square feet of Smaaash Sports Centres within the mall, where all categories of Olympic sports, summer and winter included, could be played. Had the issue gone through and had MOA agreed to my legitimate request, things would have been different for Smaaash. Every time I had a big dream, I had fallen flat on my face.

There was no time to waste and I had to figure out how to get new investors on board. We appointed a Mumbai-based investment banking firm. However, the investors were less than enthused about the revenue per square feet; declining existing same-store sales year-on-year; declining EBITDA margins; and uncertainty over future sponsorships because other than Star and Pepsi we were unable to attract new sponsors. In addition, they did not think that the equipment business was sustainable. However, we did get a term sheet from another lending institution, in fact from two of them. The team and I also met an equity fund in January 2020 and in March, they issued a non-binding term sheet for equity infusion where the rights and obligations of existing investors would be protected. However, my shares would be transferred to them at a nominal consideration of Rs 1.

If this deal went through, I would be left with nothing. The lenders would take my real estate, including the residential premises that my wife called 'home', the residential premises in which my daughter was staying with her family, and above all, my retirement home in Lonavala. My shares were at zero value and so were the efforts of the last forty years of relentless hard work. Having lost everything that I had built, this was a quintessential riches-to-rags story. For the first time, I broke down in office.

I no longer had the emotional and mental wherewithal to continue the operations. I was losing credibility with the malls with whom Smaaash was constantly defaulting on rentals, revenue share, cam and utility payments. I would be in the middle of something when the CFO would come stating that the electricity of the mall had been shut. I would ask him to give a post-dated cheque for the following Monday (usually the best collections were Saturday and Sunday) and assuage them.

A landlord for our two malls in Delhi gave me the impression that he could take things to the next level if need be. But they were still better than the ones in which there was foreign ownership, who were ruthless and uncompromising. They only understood the language of money. Pleading with them was an uphill task. Our two cash cows—the conference centre and the upscale hookah bar had shut down, and in December, we lost possession of three malls—two in Delhi and one in Bangalore, which were a part of the acquisition made by us. The loss of these malls meant a loss of 38 per cent of revenue and 42 per cent of the EBITDA of the bowling company that we had acquired. Then, the beverage company stopped its sponsorship revenue. While Star was still meeting its commitment on sponsorship, the signal was clear—that on expiry of the contract in 2020, they would not renew it.

Taking all the factors into account, I realized that it was worth living the life of a pauper, rather than facing such a plethora of challenges day in and day out. After all, these were not the only challenges I was facing. Our account with the lenders had become a non-performing account (NPA) and according to their claims, we had defaulted not only on the principal amount but also on the interest for a continuous period of six months. I used to argue with my lenders that the term sheet had captured the fact that 50 per cent of the loan was to be paid from the proceeds of an IPO which we tried. The idea had their approval in writing, but it did not work out.

How was the company to make payments when its EBITDA was barely Rs 30 crore (if we remove capitalization of expenses?) They were in no mood to listen. I believe that the ILFS crisis had hit them very hard and the market was agog with rumours about them going through a liquidity crunch. They had completely truncated the organization of the NBFC and were negotiating a sale of their broking and wealth management businesses. In their wisdom, they decided to transfer the business to their very own asset restructuring company (ARC).

In a way, I was relieved. I would no longer have to deal with their chief legal officer and the Malayali gentleman who would call me at the most unearthly hours. Our conversations disturbed my wife and I would calm her down by telling her that I would save our real estate. But frankly, I had no idea how I was going to do that.

Initially, the meeting with the ARC went smoothly. The two officers in charge—especially the one who was ex-McKinsey—were extremely sensible. His only interest was in finding solutions and resolving the impasse.

Around January 20, when we were meeting investors, my chairman asked me to come to Dubai. He had an investor lined up for $50 million. Having suffered from several false promises I asked the chairman if he was sure. I got a long telephonic lecture as to how in JP Morgan and Dubai World, he had got investors who helped companies in distress, create value. I had no other option but to believe him.

In January, I flew to Dubai. There was an intermediary who had worked in a reasonable position in a Dubai-based bank and was respectable. During our conversation, I got to know that he had been offered the role of the head of Share Khan's Dubai office, a role that did not materialize.

The intermediary introduced me, in a small 1,000 square feet empty office, to a portly South Indian gentleman by the name of Raja. Raja assured me that he could read faces and that I was a genuine person, and agreed to invest $150 million in Smaaash. That very day, we drew up an investment agreement. I had to transfer a processing fee of $4,00,000 which the intermediary and my chairman encouraged me to do. In fifteen days, the fund would be in my account . . . or so I was told.

Fortunately for him and unfortunately for us, Covid-19 hit India. Back then, I was in Hong Kong chasing Raja a month after his committed date. Everyone was wearing masks and the hotel insisted we wore masks as well. Raja told me on the evening of the 15th that employee attendance in the bank was low and that he would stay back in Hong Kong to complete the transaction. The person from my Dubai office and I decided to leave Hong Kong.

On reaching Mumbai, we received a term sheet from the private equity fund and we distributed it to all the investors on 18 March. This term sheet was going to spell my doom. It was around that time that India's prime minister, Narendra Modi, announced a nationwide lockdown. Covid-19 would be deadlier than anyone had anticipated. It was a pandemic and the first of its kind that humanity had seen in a long time. Malls and cinemas were the first to close and soon we were restricted to our homes.

For me, it was a blessing in disguise. I would be at home and have long hours to myself to think about my future. To date, for the last forty years, I have only thought about how to solve the next problem or a set of problems. I knew that I had another decade to live at most (if I was spared in the pandemic) and I needed to think about my plans to navigate the period 2020–2030.

My business was in trouble. I had a huge debt outstanding. How would I deal with my employees during the Covid-19 period? Was there any way of solving my problems so that I could save my business *and* my real estate?

There were only questions. No answers.

16

The Covid-19 Period

The wound is the place where the light enters you.

—Rumi

March 2020–October 2021

When Covid-19 was slowly but steadily creeping into nations bordering China, I was in Dubai chasing the fraudster, Raja. Let me explain how I concluded that Raja was a fraudster. He would call us to Dubai and then fly to Hong Kong on the date I was supposed to land. He would then ask me to meet him in Hong Kong. While my chairman insisted that I pursue him, my investment banker warned me that if Raja had taken the money in advance, he was a fraud. On the other hand, my chairman's sources thought that we should not dismiss Raja so lightly. He was not a dubious character, they said, and had access to funds akin to a goldmine.

The intermediary who introduced us to Raja would exult confidently that the latter had all the money on one hand, and then he would change his mind, insisting that Raja was a waste of time. To be fair to him, at least, he was on shaky ground with Raja too, considering the man would blow hot and cold, depending on his mood. Over time, I discovered that Raja would use him much like a man Friday, making him run errands, shop for groceries and cook for him. In the meantime, man Friday continued to give me mixed signals about the availability of funds. On some days, he would be optimistic about calls between Citibank and his 'board' in sorting out payments. On other days, he would tell us that Raja was planning to buy a jet for himself!

In pursuit of Raja, I had taken nineteen trips just because my chairman had a lot of faith in him.

When I finally tracked him down in Hong Kong, Raja declared that the bank's attendance was poor as the pandemic was staring them in the face. He also gave us a few names of people who were handling his account. Since the transfer would not be possible, he would send us his location details every ten minutes for two to three hours in a row on WhatsApp. They all showed us that he was in HSBC. You see, he had access to shady means to attest his authenticity. He made us speak to various people claiming that they were from the bank. In turn, these voices at the other end of a telephone line assured us that the money was available but because of Covid-19, and in the absence of staff, transfers were difficult. For us, it was not hard to believe. After all, Raja paid for the flight tickets and hotel bookings of his entourage, consisting of the common advisor (who introduced me to him at the behest of my chairman) and two more people.

Back in Hong Kong, I did not understand the intensity of Covid-19 until I went to my regular Italian restaurant for dinner. At 8 p.m., it should have been packed, instead, I was their only customer. The newspapers were full of news of the virus. Kalpana called while I was eating, insisting that I come home. I'm glad that I listened to her. Just a day after I had departed, Hong Kong placed a ban on international flights, the first country to do so.

Back home, the fund that had given us the term sheet withdrew it, because of news of the pandemic. The gravity of the situation and the extent of the spread of the virus hit me hard in the second week of March. The footfall in malls began to dwindle to a trickle and our revenues fell by 90 per cent!

My CFO and I began to discuss the option of shutting down operations. It was then that the lockdown was announced by Prime Minister Narendra Modi. I should have been more worried about the monthly salaries and about the post-dated cheques I had foolishly issued to various malls. I should have been more worried about whether Covid-19 would strike me, and if it did, how would I restart the business. But instead, I was thinking deeply and philosophically about what the pandemic would bring, and where it would lead us all. I pondered over this singular catastrophe which affected every individual across the globe, be it China, the USA, Europe, or even India. All of us were connected in some kind of doomed cycle. Gradually, more reports began to come in: of the virus spreading across the world like wildfire through a dry forest. Countries were suspending international flights. People were dying. Every one of us would have to make vast changes to our lives. What did it all mean? You might think that the timing for this sudden burst of philosophy was bad—and you wouldn't be wrong—but I was obsessed by it.

Just four months before the lockdown, my godparent Arvind, with whom I had stayed in New Jersey, introduced me to concepts like reincarnation, *samayak* (a forty-eight-minute practice to attain equanimity and mental calmness), and *pratikaman* (repentance by confessing to sensory acts and seeking forgiveness). Arvind had always been a deeply religious person, and somehow, I was drawn towards starting to practise these principles.

I started listening to the lectures of the renowned Jain acharya, Ratna Sagar Maharaj. He was over seventy and had undergone a bypass, but his energy was that of a twenty-something youth. There was power in his speech and I felt rooted after every lecture. He had completely surrendered to the Jain philosophy and to his guru whose 'Kal Dharma', in which the soul leaves the body, took place in 1993. At the age of sixty-two, under the aegis of his lectures, I realized the importance of complete devotion and surrender to one's guru or god.

God is the manifestation of the cosmic consciousness that we are all a part of and the guru is the authorized emissary of god. Until then, I was not dedicated to either god or a guru. I was involved with my work and firmly believed that work was worship and I misunderstood what karma yoga meant. I loved my family, wife, daughter, in-laws and my godparents who were spiritually more advanced than I was. However, it was not a case of complete unconditional surrender.

It was during the lockdown that I understood how difficult it is to be born a human and how lucky we are that we do not have to worry about where our next meal is coming from. In Jainism, it is believed that human life is rare and precious and is obtained after millions of births in other forms. It is only humans and not even the *devis* (goddesses) and *devatas* (gods) who can look inward, discover their true selves, repent for sins committed, and attain the status of tirthankaras. This may sound extremely elevated, but in reality, the more I thought about it, the more I realized that so much of my life had been a push towards understanding karma and dharma and their positive implications on one's daily life.

I began to be consumed with the need to understand Jainism, to understand its philosophy and teachings. Karma, I realized, was not the punishment we associate it with but is a governing stricture for all human behaviour. Sure, it can hit you millions of lifetimes later, but it could hit you the next day too. In times of great disaster, when faith is all you have to hold on to, these things make sense. Covid-19, I began to realize, was the result of collective karma, arising from the collective actions of humanity. It was a prophecy that came true over time.

My time oscillated between Jain religious discourses and work. I was following up with Raja and my various constituents, but Raja was still giving me empty promises.

The chairman asked me to file for arbitration in Singapore as per the share subscription agreement. My wife and I told him that we did not have surplus funds to fight a legal case. However, he got a lawyer for a concessional rate of 10,000 Singapore dollars and we decided to move arbitration against him. I knew it would be of no use—and I was right. Raja would never pick up the calls from the lawyers. He was so shameless that he would talk to my wife and tell her to forget the $150 million as he had bigger plans for me. The costs built up day by day. Though my chairman insisted that we continue, I took the unilateral decision to drop the case.

One day, Raja called me on WhatsApp video and opened a Citibank App to flash his account balance which was $500 million!

He assured me that the first 50 million would go to me. He had to fulfil some formalities with the bank and once that was done, the pending transfer would follow suit. He also told me that his jet was being delivered that quarter, which would make it easy for him to travel. He claimed that he was doing something big with China and the US governments. Honestly, I was relieved.

In the meantime, my other constituents—the malls—began to move against me. A Delhi- and Gurgaon-based mall—the same man who had flashed a gun at me during negotiations—now filed an arbitration suit. I was not present for all the hearings and I did not want to make any fresh financial commitments till I got the funds promised by Raja. The other group of malls had gone one step further and had hired a person who had criminal charges against him to remove our games from the malls in Indore, Navi Mumbai and Chandigarh. I could not fathom the urgency as the Covid-19 lockdown was in full force.

Almost all games and bowling alleys were removed, destroyed and rendered useless for any further use. I do not know how they even got permission to do so at the peak of the lockdown. Persistent calls to the mall management went unanswered. To be fair to them, I owed them money of approximately 3 crore. Despite that, they took a call during Covid-19 to act both ruthlessly and covertly, thus exhibiting the dangers that small and medium businesses face at the hands of heartless foreign funds. The landlord in Kamala Mills demolished the entire conference centre, hookah bar and go-karting track so that his nephew's wedding could take place there. Luckily, the other mall owners were patient and in their heart of hearts, they had the confidence that I would come back stronger.

I did not ignore my lenders. We went back and forth on Zoom calls during the lockdown and once things opened up, I met them in person to assure them their money was safe. With their permission, I appointed a UK-based investment banking firm to find potential buyers for Smaaash. I wanted to deepen my spiritual knowledge and not restart Smaaash. They agreed and I was always told by the CEO of the ARC that he had no problem reducing and restructuring the debt of the operating company so long as the holding company's debt, which was equivalent to the value of properties, was cleared. That was the time when one of the two operating officers of the ARC, an ex-McKinsey guy, was extremely practical.

In the meantime, we made three offers through the offices of the investment bank appointed by us. Without evaluation, they were relegated to the dustbin on the pretext that the bidders were my nominees. There was a shareholder who had a large lottery business in Chennai and who had started an online real-money gaming company (now banned by the government of India), and he showed preliminary interest. We sent the required documents and they asked me to call him two days later. I followed up persistently, but to date, they have not had the courtesy to even return my call.

The possibility of selling Smaaash arose with a company that provided family holidays on a time-share basis. It was an associate of one of the largest companies in the automobile sector. They showed keen interest in acquiring Smaaash and said that they would do it only in 'partnership' with me. We drew up a term sheet in consultation with their CEO and one of the trusted lieutenants of the group who was staying in Karjat during Covid-19 times. Everything was decided and a documentation room was created for the same.

I heaved a sigh of relief because I would not have to convince an ARC as the buyer had substantial clout. We were to start the diligence call at 10 a.m. on Monday and were waiting for the proposed buyers to send the VC link. At 9.30 a.m., I called up the CEO who in turn asked me to call the 'other' gentleman, the confidante of the group. When I called him, I was told that the PR firm of his group was of the view that the merger would not be perceived well by the minority shareholders.

I was stunned. I did not know how to react. When my wife asked me what happened, I had nothing to say and I thought I would get a heart attack.

I was disillusioned and I did something antithetical to not only the teachings of Jainism, but also business insight. I made a knee-jerk decision under stress and impulsively wrote an email to all my employees, telling them that I would not be restarting Smaaash. It was a way to let them know that they were free to look for other jobs. The Delhi head and his cohort—the head of marketing —leaked this information to a prominent business newspaper.

The newspaper lapped up our story of business failures and sensationalized it.* My photograph was splashed across their front page and all hell broke loose. There were continuous calls from malls and shareholders. I told them that I did not want to live with the guilt of people being unemployed in the hope that Smaaash would revive. Our ARC also got aggressive and during Covid-19, they sent an entire posse of officers to take possession of our Lonavala house, thinking it would be empty.

However, my daughter, son-in-law, and granddaughters with their cousin and his family had been there since the onset of the Covid-19 lockdown. I was in a panic. It was 21 July and I had just turned sixty-one a few weeks ago. It was the first time in my life that I sought the intervention of our family lawyer. She was a gem of a lady, and she lost no time in appointing an expert in the field. She also immediately spoke to the ARC team telling them that they could take a symbolic possession but not a physical one. Next, we filed a case in the debt recovery tribunal (DRT). Then, they came to my residence and the vacant residence in which my daughter had lived in

---

* Vibhuti Sharma, 'Popular game arcade Smaaash shuts down as pandemic hits business—sources', Reuters, 22 September 2020, https://www.reuters.com/article/world/asia-pacific/popular-game-arcade-smaaash-shuts-down-as-pandemic-hits-business-sources-idUSKCN26D0T3/

Mumbai (as everything was mortgaged to them) and pasted notices on our doors. One time I was out of town and my wife was alone and I requested them to come the next day, but the officer of the ARC threatened me with dire consequences if he was not given access. He added that he would be forced to talk to our society and the local police station. Finally, we agreed that they would not go inside the house and would paste the notice on the door.

My lawyer advised us to remove the notices as soon as the team left. Since the matter had now come down to our homes, I was also advised to change my lawyer to someone who was defending the biggest default by a telecom services company, and afterwards to another gentleman who was an erstwhile director of a nationalized bank. The biggest regret I have is in changing lawyers. My first lawyer should have been my final one. The last lawyer kept on increasing the number of lawsuits in various courts and initially advised a liberal settlement that never materialized. Today, my relationship (I do not even know if I had one) with the ARC is acrimonious and beyond repair. I have had a fair share of problems with YES Bank and SIDBI but they have been manageable.

At one point, I did not know the future of Smaaash or how to save the houses or what would happen to my family if all was lost. There were only questions with no clear answers.

As countries and governments began to stabilize after long months of Covid-19-induced emergency, I knew that I had to take a decision. Travel was difficult between countries but I thought to myself, '*Der hain par andher nahin* (It's still not too late). God wants Smaaash to survive.'

The next day, after taking a Covid-19 test, I took the flight to Dubai. Raja had arrived in his private jet from London with his 'team'. 'He flies in his own jet and I'm sure he will now pay up,' I thought.

That evening, Raja invited me along with a group of his friends from the tech sector to sail on his yacht. We were given the honour of inaugurating the yacht. The next day, Raja returned the $4,00,000 that we had doled out to him. He then showed his bank balance of $42 million with a Dubai-based bank. He asked me to meet his relationship bankers at two banks who claimed that he had substantial balances and that pending some formalities on money laundering, the money would be released. It is important to note that I met these relationship managers—one in the branch of a UAE bank and the other in the branch of a US-based bank who asked me to meet her late afternoon at a café.

Today, I realize that these officials were fake, but how were they seated at bank offices is a question that still bothers me. I have never found them on LinkedIn or social media. By August 2020, I put an end to my pursuit of Raja. Yet, he would call and promise me the moon.

I was in a mess and I knew it. Roadblocks were plenty and solutions were none. The ability to surrender to the supreme lord was not something I knew because my knowledge of religion was superficial.

What should I have done? Why couldn't I save Smaaash? Could I save the house? It was all about me, my ability and salvaging my ego. I did not have the awareness that we are subject to the reaction of our accumulated karma and are always at His mercy. We are nothing but puppets and the strings are pulled by our karmas.

This lack of realization made my life extremely difficult and for the first time in sixty-odd years of my life, I could not sleep at night. Listening to Jain *pravachans* (discourses), which had brought me so much peace earlier, didn't help at all. My brain would lapse into endless analyses at night. What people told me went unheard and I was only obsessed with what would happen next.

17

Post-Covid-19 Revival . . . the Blockbuster Period

Goodbyes are only for those who love with their eyes. Because for those who love with heart and soul, there is no such thing as separation.

—Rumi

October 2021—April 2022

I analysed the situation thoroughly and concluded that the only way to save the houses was to restart the company by eliminating its shortcomings. I thought through the following:

- How do I get to a cost of Rs 1,500 per square foot on fit-out costs?
- How do I get to a cost of Rs 2,000 per square foot on equipment cost?
- How do I make the centre more appealing and pleasing to the eye?

In all this, the only decision I did not take was whether to continue with F&B.

At the outset, a group of ten people was rehired—three operation heads for north, south and west India. I hired one member of the accounts team and two assistants, a junior marketing associate, and a design head, while I outsourced HR to the agency that had remained with us through thick and thin.

Secondly, I sold some of our heirloom jewellery and paintings. I owned a collection of Lord Ganesha paintings created by contemporary masters. It was just post Covid-19 and I got Rs 7 crore for a Rs 20-crore portfolio. However, I was fine with it, as I urgently needed funds to restart the centres.

The businesses I had started in the past had never met this disastrous fate. I was always willing to work hard to be successful, and for me, restarting Smaaash was a holy event. Every brick I laid was akin to a 'punarstapam', a resurrection of sorts or a 'shilaanyas', laying the brick of a temple.

Once there was an influx of funds from the sale of my property, I set up a three-member team of research and development comprising the third-in-command in the pre-Covid-19 years of Smaaash, along with two engineers, one of whom was an existing employee and the other a fresh recruit. Within seven days, we came up with eight to nine new products that had a relatively low cost. The expensive German components were substituted with Indian components. They were manufactured by passionate engineers from prestigious engineering colleges.

Next, we contacted landlords including those who had ruthlessly ousted us. One thing in common with all the landlords was that revenue sharing would now be converted into fixed rentals as no one was willing to waive off rentals during the Covid-19 pandemic. This meant an increase of 75 per cent to 100 per cent for fixed rent and that would have to be paid irrespective of the revenue earned.

I did not want to take undue risks and I took a call to shut certain centres like DLF Cybercity knowing full well we would be out of Gurugram. However, a 300 per cent rent increase proposed by the DLF management was something I could not risk. Certain low-yielding centres such as Bhopal, Mysore, Siliguri, and two smaller centres in the neighbourhood malls of Hyderabad, were shut. We moved all our equipment to the more profitable centres. Eventually, we were removed from two malls in Gurugram, and one each in New Delhi, Chandigarh, Amritsar, Bhopal, Indore and Navi Mumbai. When we commenced operations at the Bangalore mall, the landlord increased our deposit and rental by 280 per cent! This was even though the only footfall in the mall was because of Smaaash. Out of sheer disgust and anger, I decided to move out.

Apart from this, other problems created roadblocks. There was massive pilferage of liquor bottles in centres across the board. Plus, I had to rebuild my presence in all these cities, the biggest challenge being Mumbai. I was convinced the landlords would not accede to my request for Mumbai. I had rejected a site in Andheri six to seven years ago. Now, I requested the broker to help me get that site if it was available. It was. However the landlord never returned the broker's calls. Frustrated, I went to the Govanis, my landlords of the first Smaaash Centre at Kamala Mills.

To my surprise, they agreed to continue with the Mumbai centre on the following terms: 1) a rent of Rs 60 lakh per month or 20 per cent revenue share, 2) an increase in deposit, 3) clearance of the past overdue rentals by buying their shares. He was right in demanding this, as we had a buy-back clause in the share-purchase agreement signed with the landlord. I instinctively told him that I had 20 acres of land in Pachghani whose value was Rs 2–2.5 crore per acre and this would adequately secure his receivables. Lastly, we signed an arbitration agreement and renewed the lease agreement.

In January 2021, work started in Mumbai. The entire place was shrouded in gigantic cobwebs. The arcades were in a state of disarray and almost all the go-karts were in a sorry state and the double-decker track had been demolished. I had always regarded Mumbai and Kamala Mills as my karma bhoomi as this was where I started my first centre.

Fully aware of the big risks after parting with all of my residual assets, I was reopening Smaaash with determination and noble intentions. I never thought about what would happen if all was lost in the pursuit of my goals.

Gradually, I started expanding the project team in Mumbai. In Chandigarh, we identified a high-street space above a car showroom. The rest of the five-storeyed building was empty, but they were willing to give a lot more support by taking up the bulk of lease improvement expenses.

Eureka! I had the equipment and they were paying for fit-outs. This became the new model for Smaaash! A mall would contribute anywhere between Rs 1,500–Rs 2,500 per square foot towards fit-out costs and we would incur the rest.

The euphoria was high. Cinema was dead. OTT had replaced the multiplex culture. But in March 2021, Covid-19 struck yet again, this time with far greater intensity. But I did not lose heart and continued working and put up a post on LinkedIn that we were on the lookout for space between 20K and 100K square feet. The post made it abundantly clear that we needed support of Rs 1,500 –Rs 2,500 per square foot.

Several inquiries poured in and I reconnected with an old consultant who had given us two spaces—one in Jaipur—and the other in Gurugram Oyster Park. He said he could introduce us to several landlords and they started our journey to replenish the centres we had lost. When Covid-19 subsided in 2021, malls and offices were still closed. However along with my team, I started to visit various malls. Our focus was north India and we met mall owners and signed up with several properties. We were slow in execution as we earned and then spent. Additionally, there was Mumbai that had to be brought back to its feet.

Whilst restarting most of the malls was relatively easy, the Hyderabad Inorbit mall and Gurugram Oyster Park were tedious. Hyderabad wanted us to carry out major renovation and content change. On their part, they were right, as their centre like others, was dilapidated and looked unwelcoming. It was a monstrous expense. And yet with the credit from vendors, I took the risk and renovated the entire place. On completion, it looked like a spanking new futuristic zone.

By then we had reintroduced F&B. We increased the strength of R & D to sixteen people, while our old contractor resumed his services. Our newly introduced eight to nine products passed the prototype stage and we started incorporating them in our Hyderabad centre.

The response to the change was overwhelming and we were doing 250 per cent more business than pre-Covid-19 years! Our bowling alley was an artistic showcase with its blue light which has now become our signature design for the subsequent bowling lanes.

The second challenging venue was the Gurugram Oyster Park which was in the hands of an NCLT-appointed resolution professional (RP). As the promoters of Oyster Park had defaulted to the extent of approximately Rs 2,000 crore, I was convinced that bankruptcy laws had become useless. Resolution professionals and lenders have unlimited powers and work for personal benefit and gratification, as opposed to the benefit of the corporation. This applies to all resolution professionals whether independent or belonging to a reputed firm. They are not interested in the few lakhs that they make as an RP. Their vested interests lie in deals where they can generate a profit for themselves for which they form a small coterie.

Through *'saam-daam-dand-bhed'*, an age-old Indian idiom that signifies 'by all means irrespective of morality', we were able to resolve the issue. However, the go-karts and go-karting tracks were in a disastrous condition. The redesign and restructuring of the go-karting track alone cost us an astronomical fee. Despite the expense, I left no stone unturned to make the centre look aesthetically phenomenal. Soon people came in hordes and returns were up by 100 per cent at this centre.

DLF did not believe we would be successful in Noida and they wanted us out. We put our foot down and said that we would not vacate a centre where the agreement was in place. We had to give away 4,000 square feet but not pay any rent for the Covid-19 period, as the floor on which we were located (at the food court level) had to be shut because the roof of the multiplex had caved in. The DLF Centre was also repaired and renovated and over six months did 350 per cent more business than pre-Covid-19 levels.

By May 2022 we had opened the following centres:

1) Kamala Mills, Mumbai, September 2021*
2) Inorbit, Hyderabad, June 2021*
3) MBD, Ludhiana, December 2021*
4) Pavilion, Ludhiana, June 2021
5) DLF, Noida, July 2021*
6) Oyster Park, Gurugram, July 2021*
7) Nexus Mangalore, July 2021*
8) Vishal Mall, Madurai, July 2021*
9) Korum, Thane, September 2021
10) DB City Mall, Gwalior, January 2021*
11) Curo High Street, Jalandhar, June 2021

12) R City Mall, Mumbai, Dec 2021
13) Ambuja City Center Raipur, June 2021
14) Amanora Mall Pune, August 2021
15) Regalia Mall, Bhubaneshwar, August 2021
16) Berkley Square, Chandigarh, August 2021
17) Airai Mall ,Gurgaon, Dec 2021*
18) Hotel Radisson Blu Dwarka, Delhi, March 2022**
19) Z Square Mall Kanpur, May 2022

(*Indicates centres opened in Smaaash Entertainment Pvt Ltd where the ARC was the lender; ** indicates new centres that were opened to replace lost areas in Delhi and Gurugram.)

True to my intention to pay up, I first started centres under SEPL so that with an influx of cash flow repayments could start. It took me till the end of March 2022 to consolidate the position of my company in terms of my stated objective of increasing revenue and profitability.

Though we were marginally more than one-third of the pre-Covid-19 space, we were now making roughly 75 per cent more EBITDA than we ever made pre-Covid-19. This was without two branches of our revenue sponsorship and equipment sale. Sponsorship went straight to the P&L account and our net margins on equipment sales were 50 per cent of the cost of goods sold.

Many people had advised me that the concerned ARC was known to play games and the cash-cow centres should be opened in a new company so that the ARC would not be able to do what they could. But I was committed to doing the work honestly and it was as sacred as rebuilding a temple, so there was no question of cheating my lenders or shareholders. It was something I had never done in my entire life.

I kept all my constituents: lenders, and shareholders abreast of Smaaash 2.0. I had a letter from the Edelweiss management team congratulating me for the turnaround of Smaaash. As far as my properties were concerned my extended family had taken the responsibility to settle the same with the ARC, since they felt I was too soft and the situation needed a stern hand.

In December 2020, when major centres had not even started, we gave a proposal to the ARC to settle the debt at Rs 110 crore payable over four years. Plus, another Rs 60 crore was payable at the time of the IPO which meant paying the entire principal amount of Smaaash. The only write-off was the accrued interest of Rs 60 crore. They kept on delaying their response to the proposal.

Then in January, they came up with a new precondition that I should withdraw all cases. Much against the wishes of my family and advisors I did so. And still, there was no response.

Then came April 2021 and the worst wave of Covid-19 began. It was so harsh that people in their prime were dying. I was scared. My lawyers went to the offices of ARC and expressed a fear that with such severe Covid-19 onslaughts, and therefore uncertainty, we should let a big four firm arrive at sustainable debt levels. In normal times, any proposal was acceptable, but these were abnormal times and hence I needed protection. I did not want to default again. They agreed and I appointed a big four audit firm recommended by the ARC to determine sustainable debt that the company could repay. They came up with a figure of between Rs 80–108 crore as the sustainable debt.

In October, I along with my lawyers and shareholders had a meeting attended by an ex-IDBI official who was the number two person in ARC. I still have the handwritten note from one of their employees, a lady who wrote as per dictation. On 21 October 2021, we agreed to a Rs 90 crore one-time settlement to be payable no later than one year. If it was delayed beyond six months it could carry an interest rate of 11 per cent.

We agreed and left the room—only to be called back by the ARC CEO stating I had misled his officials! How could I have possibly misled a senior official with over forty years of experience in debt restructuring? I asked him and he replied that if I argued he would walk out so I kept my mouth shut. I remembered the prophecy of my advisors who told me to have the ARC under my thumb and start new centres in a brand new operating company. I should have listened to them. Now, I was under their control and the bulk of the centres restarted were in SEPL, where there was an astronomical outstanding of Rs 220 crore plus interest from the Covid-19 period.

Seven days later in November, we agreed to a figure of Rs 220 crore payable from the proceeds of an IPO at the end of twenty-four months. That amount was to carry a rate of 10 per cent interest. This was not justified as the Rs 108 crore that had gone into the American operations had gone bust. Almost all centres of the erstwhile bowling company had ceased operations, as they were in malls that were hostile to us.

I thought to myself that if I could grow to generate Rs 100 crore (60 per cent of which we had achieved) EBITDA, with my proven low-cost advantage, Smaaash could be valued at Rs 2,000 crore!

It was agreed that they would send me a letter of offer. November rolled past and before I knew it, we were in February 2023. By now umpteen calls, reminders, and follow-ups had been done. On 17 February, they sent a proposal which was valid for two days. They had taken four months to send the letter and expected me to reply in two days.

I had seventy-two shareholders and family members who felt upset that I was willing to sacrifice everything for the sake of Smaaash. This was the beginning of a rift in the family. Even younger members of the family, whom I had helped when I had the money, had no qualms about disrespecting me.

As soon as I got the proposal, I requested ten working days. I also set up a meeting with their CEO that they had asked for a payment of Rs 250 crore, and requested them to lower it to Rs 220 crore. I said that since I had sacrificed my last asset for the sake of Smaaash and repayment to ARC, and because we were not operational for the last two years on account of Covid-19, could we please stick to Rs 220 crore.

The CEO asked me to send a corresponding email which I did from the car after the meeting with him. For the next thirty days, I followed up with calls, SMS, WhatsApp and several emails. 'Sir, please respond' was my plea.

I thought that the worst was behind me but was it?

18

The Eye of the Storm

Be patient where you sit in the dark. The dawn is coming.

—Rumi

May 2022–April 2023

This sounds strange to write, and slightly tone-deaf, but in all honesty, the period from the onset of Covid-19 in March 2020, to May 2022, was most satisfying for me. During Covid-19, I learnt albeit superficially, about karma. Moreover, according to the Jain religion, karma is supreme when it comes to determining how one's life unfolds. While the ups and downs are predestined—how you react to it is entirely in your hands. I had taken the bold stand of restarting Smaaash and putting my last resources into it. I went to the extent of encashing my LIC policies. I was confident that in eighteen months, we would have a run rate of Rs 8 crore per month EBITDA. The plan was in place and it was supported by three other brands that I was planning to create in addition to Smaaash.

They were:

1) WAR, which used real guns and virtual bullets. Here the player was in a war-like situation. It was a call of duty when virtual bullets would hit the player and with the help of software, we created various war scenarios. Many group games were also created for adults as well as children. Drones and drone warfare would also be introduced in this format.

2) The Jurassic ERA was the recreation of a time, from the creation of the universe in the Big Bang to the evolution of the dinosaur era. Finally, what led to the extinction of the dinosaurs? This would include multimedia, electronics and robotics to make it a realistic experience.

3) The City of Joy was crafted to foster bonds between parents and children of all ages. It was based on the concept of play as described earlier and AI and robotics. It would be a game changer for the family where one not only plays but also learns how play affects the quality of life and EQ.

4) Sanathan Sanskar and Playground of God was my favourite, where we would introduce gods and goddesses as super humans in the Marvel and DC style. Why should our children only be exposed to the superheroes of the West when we, the cradle of civilization, had our very own gods who were the supreme superheroes? Sanathan Sanskar, and Playground of God, spread over 4,00,000 square feet was to be my swan song.

For each of these projects, properties were identified in Delhi, Mumbai, Gurugram and Chandigarh. The landlords were extremely keen to support us financially. I also identified Saudi-based entertainment company that was selling used rides, and a local rides manufacturer, with whom orders were placed. Most of the payments were done in advance and only freight, import duty and approximately Rs 3–4 crore were remaining to be shelled out.

The surge of confidence and excitement was immense within my team. I always told my team Smaaash was 'blessed by god' and that is why we were able to revive the business. At sixty-two, people known and unknown to me lauded my hard work and persistence. My LinkedIn account is a testimony of the same.

The rollercoaster was on its way up. Things were going smoothly and I had never been happier. This was my third business revival. We expanded the project and design team, as well as R & D to innovate more products. We were on a roll when it came to day-to-day operations, but criticism from the past that I was not a good manager, coupled with pressure from the family to focus on creativity and let a CEO take the operational control of the business, led to the appointment of a CEO for Smaaash.

The new CEO's career-defining achievement was Mumbai airport in 2008. According to him, all the great retail experiences, product placements, and visual merchandizing were his doing. Since 2008, he had been a freelancer and had taught in some unrated management schools. I took him under my wing and taught him the business. Once he knew the business and was comfortable, the first thing he did was to sideline my operational heads. As a result, the heads of Delhi and Punjab quit in disgust. But I had given my word that I would not burden myself operationally. After all, my hands were full with work on the project, R & D, and cash flow management.

The newly-appointed CEO gave several interviews in which he blatantly lied that Smaaash was going to invest Rs 450 crore over two years! Its repercussions were disastrous. The ARC felt that I had money for business, but I was not paying them. I wish they had verified the statement with me. My account and the core team were fully aware of how I was struggling with the cash flows. Forget Rs 450 crore; borrowing Rs 40,000 was a challenge for me.

In May 2022, NCLT, Mumbai (National Company Law Tribunal), categorized Smaaash as an insolvent company and a resolution professional from a prominent firm was appointed. In effect, the current board of directors was suspended and I lost my powers of managing the firm. I was so shell-shocked that it hampered my speech. I started to stammer and stutter, and my atypical Parkinson's was beginning to take a toll.

Despite my condition, I immediately sought a meeting with the CEO of the ARC. In no uncertain terms, I was told 'You are only interested in creating shareholder value and you have not paid for four years'. As I was struggling to speak, I told him that I would send a detailed reply on email. Subsequently I wrote to them stating:

— Our issue at NASDAQ which was approved by the lender had bombed. When the loan was given, it was evident that proceeds of an IPO or any fund raised, would be the ONLY source to clear such a large repayment of 50 per cent of the loan.

— Our cash flow had been compromised and they were fully aware of our outstanding operational liabilities as a big four firm had been appointed by them to monitor the cash flows of the company.

— For two years, the business was shut due to Covid-19 and we lost our presence in many malls. Further, it had to be restarted so that we could create value and attract investors.

— They were abreast of every situation and approved all my actions of reviving the company. The CEO of the ARC told me orally several times that he would not do anything to the company. However, there would be no concessions on the real estate that had been mortgaged.

— I had taken every step to scrape the barrel and gave them proposals aggregating 160 pages, over fifteen months, including the last one where I asked only for a concession of Rs 30 crore.

Everyone knew that it was only through a sale of equity that I would be able to repay the debt. If the company was profiting we would be able to attract capital. There was no other way.

What was happening now was a stab in the back. The CEO of the ARC changed his stance, saying, 'We need a down payment of Rs 50 crore . . . we don't trust you.'

I was too dumbfounded to even react. What had I ever done to shatter their confidence when the business was so brilliantly revived!

And yet, I assured all my landlords that it would be business as usual . . . there could be delays but I would honour all commitments.

On the advice of our lawyers, we went to NCLT to argue that we were not given a chance to present our case to them. After all, both parties must be heard in the event a company has to be admitted for insolvency. We were by no means insolvent. We were tight on resources as the business had been rebuilt, and very shortly, we would be able hold an IPO.

That is when I realized that the judiciary is extremely pro-lenders and wields an iron fist when it comes to defaulters. The lenders gave a figure of Rs 450 crore outstanding. I am yet to understand how principal + interest + penal interest could go to such an astronomical figure as Rs 450 crore! They would never provide their calculations until a much later date.

The court heard all parties and agreed in our favour on the precondition that we deposit with the court a sum of Rs 30 crore to prove our bona fides. I had just restarted the company, created Rs 50 crore consolidated EBITDA—the highest in the history of Smaaash—without any sponsorship or game sales, sold my last assets to fund the restart of the company, and above all eradicated all the ills that we saw in Smaaash 1.0. Even in dud locations like Chandigarh, our sales would be more than what we did in a prime location. To be fair, our lawyers never argued this point and it appeared that no one was interested in my side of the story.

How was I going to raise Rs 30 crore? A gentleman who had helped me during the Harshad Mehta scam came to my rescue and gave me Rs 10 crore. I went to many ex-employees of SSKI and Share Khan and only one person helped with Rs 50 lakh. The rest were just apathetic to my misery.

I was crestfallen. During my golden period, I had helped many financially. Now, those very people refused to answer my calls and ignored my text messages. It was only when I heard a statement on YouTube from a learned person that I started seeing things from a different perspective. 'Once you have given something to someone you must forget about it and if they do not respond/or return the favour you have no right to feel bad about it.' The statement gave me strength as it shattered my ego and I told myself that I am a *bhikshuk* (a seeker of alms)—I can only request and not demand.

Those with whom I shared filial bonds would give vague reasons for evading my calls. Right till the very end, as a bhikshuk, I kept requesting people I had worked with and had benefitted from the association, and those who had benefitted enormously, to extend support in my darkest hour. My calls went unanswered and my WhatsApp messages were read but not responded to.

My problem was magnified when the resolution professional (RP) from the prominent firm asked me to meet his colleague.

He was a gentleman who headed their corporate practice. According to the RP, he was likely to get the assignment for fixing the valuation of Smaaash for potential buyers. I met the colleague in a coffee shop in Mahim which was his *adda* and he explained the process very nicely.

He told me that the RP and he would be on my side provided:

— I gave him a payment of Rs 65 lakh over six months.
— I would have to appoint an individual to negotiate with the ARC for a hefty fee which would run into crores.
— I would have to appoint a forensic auditor to defend myself against any wrongdoings in the company at the cost of Rs 50 lakh.

The next day he asked me to meet at the auditor's office located near Bombay Canteen in Kamala Mills. The colleague wanted me to appoint the audit firm as a forensic auditor for a rich and royal fee of Rs 50 lakh. The term rich and royal will be well understood when the RP appointed a forensic auditor for Smaaash for just Rs 2.5 lakh. Clearly the deal was structured to benefit the colleague and the RP.

The subsequent day, we met the person who was supposed to fix my problem with the ARC, at Sofitel in Bandra Kurla Complex, Mumbai. First, he claimed enormous influence over them and when I asked him what he had done so far with them—I was told that a Rs 20-crore loan was settled for Rs 15 crore. I did not know if it was the truth or otherwise, but I was not impressed.

Just to buy time, I gave the colleague Rs 5 lakh that was sent to the office of the forensic auditor we were supposed to appoint. He sent me the engagement letters from the debt consultant and the forensic auditors.

I was warned against the RP and his partner's trap and I bought time, and sometime around August–September, I told them that I would not be able to accede to their request. The person the RP had asked me to meet to fix the deal was calm, cool and collected and said, 'no issues'.

This incensed the RP and he declared an all-out war! The first allegation against me and the team was that we had siphoned off Rs 2 crore from the company. To harass us, a police complaint was filed in Noida, Gurugram, Mumbai and Hyderabad simultaneously. In the first two places, the case was closed immediately. In Mumbai, two complaints were filed— one in Mahim and the other at N.M. Joshi Marg. The one in Mahim was not acted upon, but I do not know the progress of the other one as I have been missing in action since May 2023. From then on, I was battling severe depression, anxiety and other physical challenges.

After that, the RP got the CEO on his side. Salaries would not be paid to people who were 'perceived' to be close to me and that included the business head, finance, HR and R & D department. The situation was such that now the CEO and his appointed officers were doing private business on the side and were siphoning off resources to the extent of Rs 10 lakh per month from the company. The Hyderabad head was openly working as a consultant for a rival company and there was no one to keep a check on their unprofessionalism.

The RP sought help from another RP, a senior partner of his firm who had been suspended from acting as RP by the statutory authorities. He acted as a de facto police inspector, treating the employees as petty criminals. Two of the finance guys' phones were taken away and their personal and professional WhatsApp messages were checked without giving any reason whatsoever. Two seniors in the finance department were suspended. On the CEO's instructions, the names of these people and those close to me were circulated by his HR head and disbarred from the centres run by them.

Much before these events commenced, I complained to the CEO of BDO, one of the large international accounting and consulting firms for which the RP and his so-called partner worked, on email. However, I got no response for nearly forty days. So, I made a phone call. From our conversation, I figured he was my classmate in Sydenham and knew my cousin brother well and I saw a sliver of hope. He apologized and said he was traveling and agreed to meet me the next day. When I called him, he told me that this was a whistle-blower's complaint (all this is evidence in an email) and his legal department had to step in. He assured me that the right action would be taken.

I trusted him. But instead of acting on my complaints, there were merciless actions taken against my team and me. Payments were withheld from vendors who had been working with Smaaash for a long time with the reason given that I, 'Shripal Sir', would make the payment. One day, we were unceremoniously thrown out of the office and access to official documents that belonged to my family and my employees were restricted.

The stress I went through was immense but work kept me going. I was determined to rebuild Smaaash even if centres under SEPL, including the one in Kamala Mills, would never be mine again.

Legally, we fought hard going right up to the Supreme Court and in all the cases we challenged the assignment of debt from the finance company to their own ARC, much against the rules set by The Reserve Bank of India. The Supreme Court was sympathetic to our case but at the insistence of the high-flying lawyers of the ARC, who demanded that we deposit Rs 50 crore. Now, short of stealing, I did everything, but I was unable to raise the resources. I did not understand why the ARC was not respecting me for restarting the operations in an extremely profitable manner.

Why were they not recognizing that the value they would get from others would be far lower than the value they would get from me? Why were they and their agents (the RP team) acting in a manner that was detrimental to the interest of the company? Why were they not recognizing that the American operation and all the bowling alley centres that we acquired had shut down? Yes, we made mistakes but having learnt from them we had turned the company around adequately. Why were they calling us 'fraudulent' and not acting on the complaint against the RP? They had not even asked us to provide evidence.

As a micro, small and medium enterprises (MSME), we employ more than 1,000 people directly and 5,000 people indirectly. At one point, our respected Prime Minister Modi-ji said, 'for us, MSME means—maximum support to micro, small and medium enterprises.' Have the actions of ARC and RP adhered to the vision of our prime minister?

Yes, I repeat, I had made mistakes, but those were genuine business failures. There was no intention to con anyone.

In life, there are prizes to be won and prices to be paid. This price was just too hard to bear. It almost cost me my life. Mentally humiliated and physically exhausted, I asked myself, was this journey even worth it?

I had tried to create a win-win situation for all. This company, the only one of its kind in active entertainment, would benefit a great deal from an IPO which would pay for all the dues and allow us to settle with the lenders. Lastly, the shareholders could walk out with profit and all the employees who supported us would benefit from ESOPs. And in turn, I could walk with my head held high. However, that was not to be. By now, the ARC had possessed all our properties, and the manner in which they did it made it evident they wanted to humiliate us.

The law clearly states that you can make a tenant vacate their property only before sunset especially if women and senior citizens are involved. However, without any consideration, on a grey evening in November 2022, a posse comprising ARC officials, a debt trustee, and six to seven police officials from NM Joshi Marg arrived at my apartment at 7 p.m. I was out of town. They told my wife to vacate our home immediately. She was stumped. She panicked and by god's grace, my son-in-law and my lawyer were there to assuage her. All my wife could carry out with her were essential documents and a few sets of clothes. The humiliation was soul-crushing and it took over a month for her to get over the trauma. This was the first time ever that she had to face something so terrible. Not the lenders, but their agents and the police behaved respectfully. The lenders intended to hurt us where it hurt most—our self-respect. While the properties were mortgaged and the courts were sorting out the matter of the property though sub judice, by hook or by crook, they chose to take possession of the property, in violation of the spirit of the law.

I flew back to Mumbai on the same night and complained to the police commissioner. I also reached out to the police through a lawyer. Sadly, they did not revert. Within three weeks our two flats on Altamount Road and the bungalow in Lonavala were also seized by them. My daughter, son-in-law, and my two innocent granddaughters had to move out as well. They lived in a rental apartment and for the next six months, my wife and I moved in with them as well, as we had nowhere to go. My son-in-law and his parents were very generous to accommodate us under their roof, though they were under no moral obligation to do so.

I took my fall graciously. However, what I could not bear was that I had fallen in the eyes of my family members. Their anger towards me was evident during the normal course of conversation. It was earth-shattering, as it resulted in ugly family spats.

19

The Storm and Its After-Effects

There is a void in your soul ready to be filled. You feel it, don't you?

—Rumi

May 2023

Despite the macabre Covid-19, I had managed to reestablish Smaaash. It was a true turnaround story and I thought that the bad times were behind me.

I was zipping down the expressway, gaining momentum at every milestone, when out of nowhere I screeched to an abrupt halt. Merciless karma punctured my pace. The company was admitted for insolvency by NCLT, Mumbai, and there would be no turnaround unless I deposited Rs 30 crore. But where was I going to get such a large amount of money?

Stress and anxiety aggravated my atypical Parkinson's. However, instead of giving up, the anxiety gave me the impetus to move ahead. I looked at the situation as an unfortunate impediment. After all, Smaaash was blessed by the gods and I moved on and made it seem as if nothing had happened.

I spoke to all my landlords and requested them not to panic. While the landlords were contributing Rs 1,000 to Rs 1,500 per square foot, there was a balance of Rs 2,000–Rs 3,000 per square foot of equipment costs. After SEPL, I only had a few centres that were smaller and not yielding much EBITDA. As it is, most of the EBITDA went into servicing the lawyers' fees.

Work came to a halt as the cash flow from SEPL was no longer available. The control of cash flow was with the RP who used it against me. Lawyers were paid Rs 9–14 lakh per hearing. For such a small company, five accounting firms including the big four were employed by the RP to comb through and make sure they found some fault or the other.

The dirty tricks department of the BDO headed by one of their partners was trying hook, line and sinker to get me incarcerated.

The term 'defaulter' is an abused word. Factors like defaulting in repayments on account of genuine business losses and fundraising not going through because of the downward spiralling market—are completely ignored. No one considered that the company had been successfully resurrected on the lender's oral confirmation. After all, in business, isn't an oral confirmation akin to a contract? Restarting a company is not admissible as a defence. The law has given carte blanche powers to RPs and lenders to the extent that they can wreak havoc in an entrepreneur's life.

My personal life was on shaky ground as my loved ones were losing faith in me and my abilities. It affected my morale once in a while, but I was mindful not to let it affect me so much that it hampered my ability to work. I moved on to creating more centres in a company that had no relations with SEPL or those that were taken over by the lenders. With laser-sharp focus and breakneck speed, new centres burgeoned in Pune, Bangalore, Amritsar, Jodhpur and Ludhiana—two more in New Delhi, two in Noida and one in Gurugram!

Soon, this frenzied ambition in my sunset years got the better of me and my health deteriorated to the extent that I had to be hospitalized. My family pleaded with me to slow down and hand over the reins of operational responsibilities. After all, we were 90 per cent of the turnover of SEPL and 75 per cent of the EBITDA of SEPL as of April 2023.

During this phase, I also completed one centre for SEPL in Barnala. The landlord was someone who had been dumped by his political bosses. However, he continued to wield political clout and when he heard about our precarious situation, all hell broke loose. Like a drunk bull in a china shop, he abused me with filthy cuss words and threatened to bump me off. It was only when I warned him that I would lodge a police complaint that he stopped harassing me.

The misdeeds of the lenders further dented my position in my family and among my loved ones. Up until then, there had been an aura of invincibility around me. Now that I was dethroned, I had lost their respect. Though it hurt me, I made sure to continue working. There is truth in the saying 'work is worship'—it was only my work that kept me going.

The 'new' Smaaash had still to be developed—two centres in Gurugram, one in Noida, two in Greater Noida, aggregating to 4,00,000 square feet . . . Moreover, a few other centres were also work-in-progress. Almost all landlords had been very kind to me thanks to our consultant who was extremely reputed. They were upset at the delay; despite that, their trust in me was very heartening. There were a few other hiccups—I lost my cool with two landlords—one in Delhi and the other in Noida. However, I apologized later. They were right as they relied on me to generate footfalls in their malls and my delay was letting them down. I was focusing on the new centres and creating multiple brands to facilitate our growth.

I was very enthusiastic about introducing new concepts created from my intuition. I was particularly excited about City of Joy, which exposed parents and children to the importance of play and the classrooms of the future that would include robots and artificial intelligence. My design team had structured it aesthetically. I was also excited about my project Sanathan Sanskar which I think would have been a big draw as the Ayodhya temple was under construction then. It had Lord Vishnu and his avatars, Lord Shiva, the birth of the universe, devis, the playground of the future, and the miraculous temples that went beyond science. A science museum was planned to encapsulate the Vedas, spirituality, ancient science and Mathematics and was called 'Ved se Vigyan tak'. There was so much to look forward to!

But as the saying goes man proposes and god disposes . . . The centres in Delhi, Gurugram and one in Kanpur had no fiscal support from the landlords. I borrowed Rs 22 crore from the unorganized market through a broker. He and his brother had made a five-star hotel at Nelson Mandela Marg in Delhi as their base. I borrowed from them with a commitment to pay in eight equal instalments over four months.

Though March, April and May were slow months and revenues were Rs 3 crore lower than projected, I was able to pay everything except the final Rs 8 crore. But when I requested a month's staggering of repayments there was pandemonium! They started abusing me and one brother threatened me with electric shocks. Later, I discovered they were powerful people with strong connections with politicians and police. I would get calls from lenders—people living in the periphery of Delhi (Haryana and Uttar Pradesh)—and their language was downright filthy. They would call me at odd hours, abuse me, and threaten to harm my family. One of them locked the restaurant of a newly opened centre in New Delhi.

My wife was petrified by these ruthless people and she put her foot down. I still remember her words: 'I have never interfered with you or your work since we got married. I have been with you through thick and thin, in sickness and health. I have borne the brunt of your flaming ambition, I have supported you and sold everything that you wanted . . . but now I have had enough. Smaaash is dead for you. We will repay these loans, and thereafter you will not be doing business.'

My wife and my son-in-law repaid the entire outstanding to these shady lenders.

I had never seen such aggression and fury within her. Her close relative told me that I had robbed my wife of the roof over her head. In a fit of rage, I moved out of the house. I told my wife that I never knew that failure would deter her confidence in me to this extent.

But was it a failure?

Three months ago, we had negotiated a deal with the largest listed online gaming company, where the liability in the current ARC of Smaaash group companies would be transferred to another ARC. That would close the chapter on the current ARC. The new ARC would then sell the assets to the listed gaming company. I organized a meeting between the CEO of the gaming company, their advisors, officials of the new ARC, and my family members. We shook hands and the deal was finalized to be completed by 31 March 2023. All of us heaved a sigh of relief.

However, the current ARC took thirty-four days to issue the non-disclosure undertaking, and to date, the information has not been passed to them. It was on this basis that I borrowed from the unorganized sector so unfortunately, the deal was dead even before it was born. I always believed in a backup. With the help of our influential investors, we found a debt fund but without knowing me or what had happened, the fund manager branded me a fraud. The head of the fund told me that they were moving ahead despite my market reputation which was that of a fraud. This was our first meeting. Despite the abuses, I made all attempts to appease them.

Hand-in-glove with the RP, the ARC filed one lawsuit after another and played all the dirty tricks they possibly could. The agenda was to paralyse us with huge legal bills that they could afford, but my growing company could not.

I had access to some agricultural land that I wanted to sell off. The papers were in the office that I used to sit which now belonged to the company that was under the RP. He refused to hand over the papers though it had nothing to do with Smaaash. They even threatened me with criminal actions and filed complaints with the Economic Offences Wing that I had done a fraudulent transfer of the brand and issued additional equity. Since the matter is sub judice, I am unable to write more. But how can someone commit fraud with his own company, a company he had resurrected? For me, rebuilding Smaaash was as pious as rebuilding a temple.

I wondered how much more harassment was in store for me. When would I be able to regain the confidence of my wife whose mental fragility and anxiety I could clearly understand?

The bleak days got bleaker when I got to know that the #2 person of the group to which the ARC belonged had vowed to a common acquaintance that they would come out all guns blazing to ensure my downfall. At first, I could not understand their animosity towards me. I felt that they thought I had money tucked away or, as the ARC head would often say, that I was sitting on a pot of gold. If this was the case, why would I borrow at high interest from the unorganized sector?

It was much later, that I stumbled upon the real reason. My family had managed to put a stay on the sale of the Lonavala property which they had surreptitiously sold to the CEO of an FMCG retail major belonging to one of the richest men in India. He was someone who had started his life as a share broker.

It was done without following the rule of law. There is a due process stated by law but they had conducted the sale behind closed doors to the CEO even though there were buyers who were willing to pay 10–12 per cent more than the quoted price. Similarly, our Lower Parel flat valued at more than Rs 35 crore was sold for a paltry Rs 19 crore.

The lifeline of the ARCs is fixed assets. Friendly valuers and auctioneers would give the ARC the desired results and ARC would simply negotiate a stipulated price with the buyer. The price could either be split into the black and white component or a quid pro quo arrangement would be made in the form of other favours to the ARC or their associated firm which would more than adequately compensate the ARC for the lower value. The CEO who was purchasing it had a wealth of more than Rs 7,000 crore. There were several ways in which one could compensate the ARC.

Unfortunately, the laws of the country do not empower courts to examine this angle. In fact, in 2023 the IT authorities raided four ARCs where parallel sets of accounts contained cash transactions of more than Rs 850 crore. All the firms to which our ARCs belonged were also raided by the IT and by the enforcement directorate subsequently. It was so unfortunate. I was being victimized for a genuine error by people who are far from being morally scrupulous. They had given the RP and the CEO carte blanche powers and I was their punching bag. I also became a punching bag for my extended family.

These injustices took a toll on me and I was in a state of shock. On 3 May, I told my wife that I wanted to be left to myself. Reluctantly, she agreed. It was time for introspection. Before I left, she told me that from next week I should have nothing to do with Smaaash. She put her foot down and said enough was enough.

What helped me during this bleak period was the knowledge of the enormous research my team and I had done on Hinduism/ Sanathan Dharma for my project Sanathan Sanskar. It was my fallback during the tough times with the ARC, RP and CEO. However, I could not face the anguish of my loved ones. I had certainly wronged them, beyond what they could bear, in fulfilling my skyrocketing ambitions. I had let down those who had been steadfast in their love and support. The guilt gave me ineffable grief and sleep eluded me for days on end.

On 8 May, I checked out of the hotel and picked up a strip of sleeping pills from a friendly chemist. That night, I decided to go to Delhi to meet some of the lenders whose harassment and mental torture had reached a different level. Some of them even visited my office with muscled goons to scare me and ensure payment. I wanted to seek postponement on humanitarian grounds. I had rehearsed my speech with them and requested my lawyer to accompany me.

I was fully prepared. I worked throughout the day, did research on an internal swarm drone for my two projects, contacted the seller, and discussed with the R & D team all the products that were in the pipeline. Things looked bright for Smaaash and I decided to fly to Delhi and meet the landlords whose projects were incomplete.

Before leaving for Delhi, I spoke to a Gujarati officer at the ARC on a WhatsApp call. He candidly told me that unless there was an advance of Rs 30 crore or I let go of the Lonavala bungalow, there was no scope for settlement. He further stated that the RP was tightening the noose on me with stricter actions as per their instructions. Masking my doubts with a laugh I asked, 'Do you want to jail me?' There was a stoic silence from his side. That was when I knew that their intentions were sinister.

That very day I was summoned to the Mahim police station in connection with 'defrauding Smaaash' to the extent of Rs 2 crore. This was my third visit to the police station because the officer-in-charge could not see me for some reason or the other. Was this an ARC tactic to unnecessarily frame me?

During the endless wait at the police station, I felt considerable pain in my head. Nausea compounded by giddiness made me ill at ease. I told the police officer who was to take my statement that I was not feeling alright. He figured something was wrong with me as my speech was incoherent and sent a police escort down to the car. When the family doctor examined me, he said that all the symptoms were stress-related.

The words of the ARC officials, my wife, my loved ones, the endless waiting at police stations, and above all those of my savage lenders from the organized as well as unorganized sector and the physical abuse, completely unnerved me.

At approximately 6 p.m., I swallowed twenty sleeping pills and washed it down with two glasses of Lizol. I passed out in fifteen minutes. My head plonked on the table with a thud. I was unconscious and in fifteen minutes my people said I was calling out to my father. My team asked for an ambulance but it did not arrive on time. So they put me in my car and drove me to Bhatia hospital.

I was delirious and so unresponsive that even when the doctor pressed my sternum (which generally is extremely painful) I felt nothing. All I wished for was death. After all, I had let all my constituents down. The ARC ignored my proposals to pay. I had to face the police as a criminal—someone who had put his last penny in the company was being accused of siphoning off funds. The dirty tricks department of the RP was working at full pace. How could a partner who was suspended for two years while doing his duty as an RP, in the case of a shipyard case, become a de facto RP?

Smaaash was my life. Every brick laid and every game installed was done with utmost piety and the grace of god. I began to feel that god's as well as my family's blessings for carrying on my job selflessly, were gone. I was terrified that if Smaaash was taken away, there would be no resources to fund myself and my family. It was at that time, albeit momentarily, that I lost my faith in god and my family, and thought that the entire universe was conspiring against me. And so, drowning in my sorrows, plagued with guilt, I took the sleeping pills. I had no intention to survive.

Epilogue

I was diagnosed with a seizure and a stroke after two days in the ICU.

This brings us back to the beginning of this book—waking up angry and frustrated. I had pushed every limit; I had pushed away everyone I loved in my life, including Kalpana. Though she was relieved and happy to see my eyes opening—I knew she was still angry. I knew that for her, Smaaash had been the last straw. It had been the only business that I had thoroughly enjoyed. I loved seeing the smiles Smaaash had brought to millions of its customers. I had wanted to die as the Walt Disney of India. Now, I would die as an unknown soul who could not do anything right.

May 2023

The next four months of my life were hell and I created hell for those around me. I was staying at my son-in-law's home. It was a task to even get out of bed. I was mired in depression and anger, and loaded with medicines, post-operative and for my mental health.

What would I do in life now that Smaaash was taken from me? I had invested time, energy and passion in rebuilding it.

Now, I had no authority or role to play anymore. For someone who used to enjoy every meal of the day, now I could barely ingest a morsel. Plunged into the deep darkness of despair, I saw no sliver of hope. Between May and November 2023, I attempted suicide thrice.

Each time, I failed.

It seemed like the pattern of my life.

Everything I touched turned to dust after that brief period when everything shone like gold.

Now, I was a failure at ending my life too.

As always, it was Kalpana who threw me a lifeline. One day, as she watched me trying to pull myself together, she gently said, 'It's okay if you cannot build a Sanatan museum. But you have gained so much knowledge in the pursuit of building one. Why don't you share that with others?' I paused to stare at her.

It was Kalpana who gave me the second life that I am leading today.

So, I restarted the study of the Vedas, Upanishads and scriptures. An anecdote from the Mahabharata stirred me from my dismal stupor:

The war of Kurukshetra was over. Lord Shree Krishna asked the great war hero Arjuna to protect his visiting Gopis from the Bhil tribes. Arjuna was happy to oblige. However, the Bhils surrounded the Gopis and robbed them of their loot leaving Arjuna incapacitated. The same Arjuna who was the son of Lord Indra, who had been bestowed with magical weapons from Lord Shiva, whose astute archery won the battle of Kurukshetra—was overpowered by the tribal Bhils.

He was flummoxed and embarrassed. How was this possible? That is when Lord Shree Krishna explained to him, 'Man thinks he is great. But that is not so. TIME is the greatest measure of success or failure. During the battle of Kurukshetra, your time

was so good that you could single-handedly overpower an army.
But time, as we all know, does not stay the same.'

I was shaken out of my reverie. When I was a successful entrepreneur, I may not have been great, but my time in the sun had been great. Similarly, now that I am at rock bottom, I am not defined by that. It is only that my *time* is not good. Why does this happen? This is a result of us clinging to everything impermanent. Our wealth, good times, success and accolades are all momentary. As the wheel of time changes, it will not even take a second for everything to disappear. This revelation softened my remorse. However, I continued to remain on a high dosage of drugs to alleviate the depression and anxiety. Occasionally, suicidal thoughts did strike me, but the intensity was on a downward slide compared to the preceding months. I was trying to rediscover my true self. I realized that we are most unkind to ourselves and self-flagellate ourselves even for minor shortcomings. It is only when we love ourselves unconditionally—aware of our strengths and weaknesses—only then can we truly love others. This also includes our love for god. In a way, being away from Smaaash was an indirect blessing. During that time, much as I had loved it, I had been moving away from my higher self. I had indulged in activities that resulted in negativity. In Jainism, our passions (*kashayas*) are divided into two categories: *raag* and *dwesh*. Raag comes from *maya* (illusion of what is right and what is wrong), and *lobha* (hungering for wealth at any cost). Dwesh comes from *krodh* (anger and physical/mental/verbal/emotional abuse) and *mann* (ego which is often mistaken for self-respect). I became an embodiment of raag and dwesh. I am a typical specimen of what Lord Krishna described as the state of humans in Kaliyuga. If I could be so insensitive why should people be sensitive towards me?

I had been in a state where I had lost all that the body and mind created—businesses, properties etc. I had done nothing for my true self, because I did not know who I was in the first place. I had never been taught the importance of that pursuit. Now, in my later years, I have discovered that path.

There is cosmic consciousness and we are all interconnected to it. Simplistically put, it is the power of all that was, all that is, and all that will be. Our role in the cosmic consciousness is to be authentic. That helps us discover our true self which is *atman*—the soul within all living and non-living things that keep it functioning whether it is an amoeba, a human being, a tree, an animal, an insect, a river, a mountain or a star. The moment the spark (soul) moves away from the body, it finds another body to give life to. Similarly, if the spark moves away from the river or the star—the river ceases to exist and the star collapses. All my life, I am fighting for what the body and the mind have created. They are nothing but illusions, whereas the atman is omnipresent, omnipotent and omniscient. But what was I doing to nurture the atman or true self.

All of us are so driven to showing off. We do not care about the light within when in essence it is that very spark that keeps us alive. Instead of looking inward and discovering our authenticity we do things to enhance our wealth, possession, power, promotion and good looks. All of us work hard to look good in business newspapers and television shows. The way our profiles look on social media is more important than self-reflection, which is the fountainhead of peace and joy.

We do not take a break to discover who we truly are. Or how we can remove our negative karma and build on the positive ones. The life I have lived is contrary to the life I should have lived. As students, we do not have respect for our teachers. As we grow older, we take our parents for granted. We set impossible goals for ourselves. The worst part is that our parents are proud of it. Our mind is constantly conditioned to demand more and more. Our tolerance is at its ebb and the need to hurt (so that we can show our power) is at its peak. If we go to the temple, it is to pray for money and power and make god a partner in our business.

This way our rewards of good and bad are equally matched and we are liberated from the journey of life and death. We want liberation from everything temporary—sadness, hate, anger, jealousy, fear, rejection and self-criticism which appears from time to time as our mind is a victim of sensory pleasures. What we need is to build a reservoir of happiness in the heart and soul. Our philosophy and religion being the most liberal have given us several ways to achieve that.

Lord Shree Krishna, in the Bhagavad Gita, states that do your work, do not shy away from responsibilities but do it as a *karma yogi*—without any expectations or rewards. Rewards or the lack of them, are determined by your karmas. Most importantly, the time when you will reap the fruit of your labour is unpredictable. That is the great big mystery of life—you never know when you are going to bear the fruit of your karma.

That, finally, is the life that I am living as I close the pages of this memoir. I have done much in my life—I have touched the highest of highs, but I have also plumbed the depths. Yes, I have been badly let down by friends, extended family (never my wife and daughter), and ex-employees, but I have learned to accept every individual as they are. They have come into my life for a reason. Whatever they did was for a reason. I should accept them as they are without rancour. Am I there? Not yet. Am I working to be there? Yes, most certainly. Sure, we want our children to be well educated, but let them first know the true essence of life. However materialistically successful you or your child is, without the knowledge of who we are and without walking on the path of guidance given in our scriptures, we are likely to drift away from the path. Just the way I did. In pursuit of discovering my true self, my atman, I hope to vanquish all the shortcomings in me even today. I do not wish to be a victim of maya/illusions any longer. I do not want anyone or their children to go through what I have been through.

Now, I seek only to surrender my ego, and to assuage the spiritual crisis I find myself in in the aftermath of Smaaash, of my attempts to die, and my many failures along the way.

Many will say, 'Oh, he is saying this now because of his circumstances'.

Perhaps they are right.

But I will always feel sorry that I let my constituents down. I have tried my best and my acts in the spiritual world are my repentance for the same. It does pain me from time to time that a company that was rebuilt to attain approximately Rs 70 crore yearly EBITDA is no longer under my control for me to pay the dues to all constituents. The only satisfaction I have is that I tried beyond my physical and mental capacities to do so. However, He has other plans for me. Living in sorrow will not help. I only hope and pray that all my constituents who trusted me are rewarded and it is the only prayer I wish to be heard.

I must end this memoir with one last line for my wife. Kalpana has never left my side, even when I pushed her to her emotional and mental limits. To her, now, I write—let our children and grandchildren learn from my experience: life's unpredictability can drive you to the nadir.

And to her, I say, with all my heart: *Thank you.*

Update (As of Diwali 2025)

I completed the memoir in February 2024. I can't believe I'm the same person. The self-development I've experienced through deep breathing techniques and meditation, in fully surrendering to Lord Shiva with all my heart and soul, is incredible.

It has led me to accept my situation with grace and gratitude. For me, meditation has turned out to be a miracle, a boon that has given me the strength to choose between reality and illusion. All those who abandoned me, I am grateful to them; they taught me to stand on my own two feet. All those who angered me taught me the art of forgiveness and compassion. All those who exercised unnecessary power over me taught me to take the power back by not reacting. And last but not least, anything that I hated taught me unconditional love. I now dare to overcome illusory fears. I have learnt to accept what I can't change, but acceptance does not mean inaction. It means fighting as an observer without being affected by the outcome.

Efforts are in your control. The results are not.

I continue to fight despite limited resources. The financial institutions and the asset reconstruction company I am dealing with are like the zamindars portrayed in the film *Mother India*. The entire system is corrupt and being misled by the lenders and their representatives because, under the law, a person who defaults is a 'crook'.

Tesla's quote—'. . . think in terms of energy vibrations and frequency' is so true. You may be low on physical energy, but my high spiritual and emotional energy have more than adequately compensated for the loss of physical energy.

I started to work here and there so that I don't have to worry about my day-to-day expenses. Finally, many of the projects are taking shape using cutting edge technologies, something that has always fascinated me. I am also working on a number of audiovisual and multimedia projects that can have a profound impact on our children and their parents. I want to do it as a charitable organization, where any individual, institution or godman can contribute to the well-being of this and the coming generations.

Our lives have been transformed by technology. Our children and grandchildren are going to be derailed by the unknown bull in the china shop—artificial intelligence. Our children will soon realize the futility of what they have learnt because someone smarter already exists. The number of professions and jobs that will be redundant is scary, and mental health will be the biggest victim. Hence, whatever I am now doing will be focused on maintaining mental and emotional equilibrium.

I live every day of my life as if it is the last day so that I don't resort to wrong actions. I accept people as they are, and if our frequencies don't match, I stay away from them. I experience in my solitude as the best time, the best thoughts and the best feeling.

Mahalaxmi belongs to Lord Vishnu—we are caretakers for some time. She stays with us because of good deeds and she finds another household when your good deeds expire. This is exactly what happened to me. What is not yours, why cry when it leaves you? We need to learn from the Tatas, Birlas and

Lalbhais about the enormous amount of benefit their wealth has reaped for society, albeit silently. They never made a display of their philanthropy.

I do not know much about the Tata and Birla families, but I know the Lalbhai family well. Even after the demise of my wife's parents, her brother, nephews and, above all, her sister-in-law have been an integral part of Shripal 2.0. The biggest lesson I have learnt from them is their ability to forgive and forget.

Today, unfortunately, people we look up to are those who are the most searched on social media, and who flaunt their wealth and affluence at every instance. We are all forgetting that our lives are meant to be dedicated to our inner journey, but sadly, we pursue the imaginary power of the senses.

Acceptance of karma and that everything that happens to you is a result of an action made in this or previous life has greatly helped me accept my new-found life of scarcity. I have realized there is no free will, and everything is as per a predetermined script. The only thing that is not fixed is one's reaction to an incident. One of the learnings I have got is not to react but to respond to situations.

Shripal 1.0 failed because he didn't understand the larger meaning of life. Shripal 2.0 is evolving, even when he knows he has lost the respect of the people around him. Many consider me foolish, and many just ignore me and don't talk to me. Does it really matter? The fact that I survived the massive downfall and can still smile and pray speaks volumes of the gods' new-found fondness for me.

I get a message from the Universe that in the coming three years I will regain all that I have lost and more. Karma is a reflection of your actions in form of reaction. The projects I am working on have given me and others confidence that the spark is intact; in fact, it is turning into a fire. My passion for technology and working with young people who are as hungry as me is helping me forge ahead. In mid-2026, my first such project will see the light of the day. Trust me when I say that my best is yet to come . . . I want to die without any financial obligations, and my success as a Karmayogi has to come because my intention is that all those who have lost money on my project because of a highly corrupt system be paid back.

Scan QR code to access the
Penguin Random House India website